—THE ORIGINS OF—
WOLVERHAMPTON WANDERERS

Patrick A. Quirke

AMBERLEY

First published 2013

Amberley Publishing
The Hill, Stroud
Gloucestershire, GL5 4EP

www.amberleybooks.com

British Library Cataloguing in Publication Data.
A catalogue record for this book is available from the British Library.

ISBN 978 1 4456 1534 9 (print)
ISBN 978 1 4456 1557 8 (ebook)

Typeset in 10pt on 12pt Sabon.
Typesetting and Origination by Amberley Publishing.
Printed in the UK.

CONTENTS

Wolves in Action
The first known photograph of Wolves in action at Molineux. (WWFC collection)

INTRODUCTION

The Origins of Wolverhampton Wanderers is essentially the record of the work and contribution of those pioneers who founded the organisation in the late nineteenth century and set it upon the road to the national and international success it has enjoyed in subsequent years. It is the story of quite ordinary young men from the backstreets of Wolverhampton who created something truly extraordinary, famous and enduring. The early years were dramatic, often turbulent, and the fledgling club nearly foundered on more than one occasion, but thanks to the efforts of the founders and supporters, it came through and survived.

It is unlikely that, at the start of it all, they could ever have envisaged what their small venture was to develop into, but their contribution and loyalty to the club has done much to shape its character, and make it something that others have wanted to be involved with for well over a century now.

The story concentrates on the part played by three men, all called Jack – Brodie, Baynton and Addenbrooke – in the emergence of Wolverhampton Wanderers, although countless others have contributed, each in their own particular and unique manner, to the way the club has grown and developed. It will attempt to detail their lives, so that readers may empathise and try to understand what motivated them: for after all, they bequeathed the world something of true value.

They gave us the Wolves.

ACKNOWLEDGEMENTS

I would like to record my sincere gratitude to the following people and organisations for all their help and assistance in producing this book:

Staff at Wolverhampton Wanderers Football Club, especially Graham Hughes, Sophie Cawthorne and Matt Grayson.

Heidi McIntosh and the staff of Wolverhampton City Archives at Molineux House, especially Alf Russell and John Everall.

Mrs Angela Lunt (head) and the staff of Brewood First School.

Mr Tony Gask and family (direct descendant of Jack Baynton).

Mr Paul Addenbrooke (direct descendant of Jack Addenbrooke).

Billy Howe – a great historian!

My wife Linda, Kevin and all the other long-suffering members of our family (who have been 'Wanderised' to distraction).

Finally I would like to dedicate this work to the memory of Meg – always there to listen and support.

1

JOHN BRANT BRODIE
The Leader of the Pack

In the middle of the nineteenth century Wightwick was a small hamlet comprising a few agricultural workers' cottages and a mill, situated about 3 miles west of Wolverhampton. At the time many people passed through Wightwick on a daily basis, either travelling along the road to Bridgnorth or working on the Staffordshire & Shropshire Canal, which passed right through the small settlement. Travellers going to or from Bridgnorth might have stopped for refreshment at the Mermaid Inn and had their horses shod at the blacksmith's forge situated next door. In the early 1860s, the blacksmith living and working at Wightwick was a local man named John Brant. Brant had three daughters, the eldest of whom was Eliza. In late 1861, seventeen-year-old Eliza became pregnant by a young iron worker from Wolverhampton whose name was Henry Hugh Brodie. At times, the father-to-be spelt his name 'Brodey', which suggests he may have had limited literacy skills. It must be remembered that this was at a time before compulsory state elementary education had been established in Britain, and so Henry's circumstances would not have been unusual. What is certain is that in the years to come Henry's appreciation and understanding of the value of education were to manifest themselves in the sacrifices he and Eliza were to make to ensure their children received good schooling.

On the 30 August 1862, Eliza gave birth to a fine, healthy son whom she christened 'John', after her father. Although Henry and Eliza married in the December of that year and the baby took his father's surname, little John Brodie kept his mother's maiden name of 'Brant' as his middle name. This was a common Victorian practice.

Like many other iron workers of the time, it seems that Henry Brodie took his little family around the area during the course of the next few years, as he sought work in any of the many small foundries around Wolverhampton. By the start of the next decade, the Brodies could be found living in a small rented house at No. 3 Haggar Street in Blakenhall, Wolverhampton. By this time the family had expanded with the addition of two younger brothers for John. Eliza was to bear ten children before her husband's death in 1889.

The area of Blakenhall lies to the south of Wolverhampton's town centre and is bounded by the roads to Sedgley (and beyond there to Dudley), the Penn Road and Goldthorn Hill. Although Blackenhall was to the west of the main coal-seams and factories that geographically defined the original Black Country district, the spread of industrialisation had changed the character of the area during the 1850s and '60s. When the Brodies moved there, Blakenhall was a rapidly developing district. Some factories were built (such as the Nyphon

Works in 1875), but by and large Blakenhall started to emerge as a residential suburb for the townspeople. On the outskirts of Blakenhall (along Goldthorn Hill and Penn Road), large mansions appeared, belonging to rich and famous industrialists such as Alfred Hickman, but there were also considerable areas around Blakenhall that were still being farmed. It was in this rich, varied and vibrant community that John Brodie was to spend his formative years.

The focal point of the emerging community in Blakenhall was the Anglican church of St Luke's, situated on Villiers Street. The land for the church was donated by local businessman and publican of the King's Arms, Dudley Road, Jeremiah Mason. Completed and dedicated in 1861, just a few months before John Brodie's birth, St Luke's had just a few parishioners when it first opened, but was frequented by greater numbers as the local population expanded. Indeed, the first illustration of the church, a painting by J. Burrows dated 1879, showed St Luke's surrounded by cornfields – a far cry from the urban parish it was to soon become. It was not long before the clergy and parishioners of St Luke's started to push for the establishment of a school wherein children might receive a basic education. Initially, it was said they would be taught to read, so that they might study the Bible; but the ongoing industrial revolution meant that a better-educated population was needed to adapt to emerging technologies. The church's benefactor, Jeremiah Mason, was called upon to provide land for the new school, and he agreed to sell several acres of open ground adjacent to the church. He charged the Diocese of Lichfield 1s 3d per square yard for the land, and by the early 1860s St Luke's schools were up and running. Jeremiah Mason's generosity was later publically acknowledged when he was given the accolade of having a street leading off the Dudley Road named after him.

With the family home in Haggar Street in close proximity to the then recently completed St Luke's church, the Brodie family started to attend divine services hosted by the Revd John Parry, and became staunch members of the Anglican community in that area. It was not surprising therefore that John and his brothers started to attend the 'large and commodious' primary school that had been built adjacent to the church, although they may have had some earlier education at St Peter's School in the centre of the town. At St Luke's elementary school, children received simple instruction in numeracy and literacy. This type of basic education was referred to as 'the three Rs' (i.e. 'reading, (w)riting and (a)rithmatic'), although in a Victorian church school like St Luke's much emphasis would have been placed on religious instruction and bible study. Interpretations of Christianity at the time included a belief that followers of the faith should be outgoing and active in their pursuit of worldly perfection and mission. In very broad terms, this manifested itself in British missionaries helping to colonise large swathes of Africa and Asia, with the intent of converting the population to Christianity. However, in terms of individuals' lives it meant working hard to be successful. Coupled with this was an increasingly popular interest in developing individual sporting prowess. This has been referred to as 'muscular Christianity' or 'athleticism', and the emergence of modern sports such as football and rugby in the mid-Victorian period could be seen as originating from it.

Unlike many of his contemporaries in the Black Country, John Brodie was fortunate that he was not expected to follow his father into the ironworks and foundries, where the work would have been physically hard and exhausting. Instead, at the age of thirteen, when he was well over the age when he could have started manual work, he stayed on at

St Luke's School. However, his new role at the school at the start of the spring term in 1875 was no longer that of pupil. On 15 January of that year, William H. Barcroft, the headmaster of St Luke's, recorded in the school logbook that 'John Brodie commenced as a monitor'. Being a 'monitor' (or as Brodie later described himself a 'pupil-teacher') meant that he had started upon a process of training to become a teacher. A teacher would instruct a monitor, while pupils practised their alphabet letters or chanted multiplication tables. He would then in turn give the same lesson he had just received to a group of younger pupils, numbering up to thirty, overseen by the headmaster. Alternatively, the head would instruct the pupil-teacher early in the morning, before school had been opened for the children. Again, they would pass on what they had been taught later in the day. Either way, the system meant that relatively few qualified teachers had to be employed to instruct an increasing number of children as the population expanded and the demand for a more educated workforce grew as Britain's industrial society continued to develop. In return for his work as a monitor, John Brodie received a small stipend from the Diocese of Lichfield and extra educational instruction. The Brodie family also knew that John would receive future financial support and recommendations from the Church when he applied to teacher training college if he were successful as a pupil-teacher.

The role of school monitor was a difficult one for John Brodie, because as a young teenager he would have been only a matter of months older than many of his charges. His youth and lack of experience meant that he would not have been accorded the same status, or respect, as the older, better-qualified teachers at the school. It is no surprise that he spent much time in the company of John Baynton, his one-time schoolmate and a fellow apprentice teacher, who had commenced work at St Luke's the year before he had. The two were to remain close friends for the rest of their lives, and were to share many memorable experiences, especially as footballers representing their adopted town of Wolverhampton.

There is little doubt that the two enjoyed messing about all through their time at St Luke's. On 10 May 1878 Barcroft complained in the school logbook that the 'teachers had not attended to their duties well this week. I have had to correct Baynton and Brodie several times within a few hours with neglect of duty.' He added that he had 'found Brodie on the floor with the boys laughing at him'.

It seems that the two boys did not have a good influence on each other, and often gave poor Harry Barcroft a difficult time. Sometimes their inattention not only affected their own classes, but those of other teachers as well, and Jack Brodie in particular gained a reputation for being extremely talkative. On 17 May 1878 Barcroft noted, 'Have been obliged to have John Brodie's class near my own owing to his continual talking to other teachers.' Even the proximity of the headmaster seems to have had little effect on Brodie's classroom discipline, as less than ten days later Barcroft reported, 'Have had to complain about the order of John Brodie's Standard (class) to little effect. He turns stupid when spoken to about it.' Poor performances in class continued throughout the year, so much so that a school inspector visiting St Luke's in December 1879 wrote of Brodie, 'He must improve or he will fail to qualify himself next year.'

The following term saw some slight improvement, but Jack Brodie seems to have developed a timekeeping problem that (along with his habit of chatting) affected his lessons: 'John Brodie has had several lessons incomplete during the week. If he were more punctual he would most likely be more successful ... He appears always to be talking.'

There is little doubt that Jack Brodie was popular with his pupils, but it must be remembered that he was only a teenager during his time at St Luke's, and it is not surprising that sometimes he acted rather immaturely. Barcroft believed that he did not manage his time well as 'he did not know how to make enough of his spare minutes, especially at the end of the afternoon', and sometimes the more rowdy elements took advantage of young Jack, causing the head to take firm action. In October 1880 he was forced to 'move John Brodie's Standard into other teachers. On one occasion the same teacher lost all control over his class, neither could he attempt to alter his style of teaching during the whole lesson.'

It was undoubtedly true that his mind was often on interests other than his academic career. Like many other young men, much of Jack's time was taken up with sport. It was as well that, with energy to spare, John Brodie was to devote himself to more productive activity, because his time at St Luke's coincided with an explosion in interest in a sport that was to eventually become a national obsession – football. The origins of the sport have been traced back to ancient China, but in more recent times the game that is now recognised throughout the world started to emerge in Britain in the mid-nineteenth century. The game and competition rules of football emerged in the 1860s and the governing body of football, the Football Association, was formed in London in 1863. In the following decades, clubs formed all over the country, and the pivotal point for the birth of Wolverhampton Wanderers as a football club may have been when the headmaster of St Luke's, 'Harry' Barcroft (who was said to be 'interested in the game'), presented his pupils with a football with which to play in the school yard. (Interestingly, Harry Barcroft was later heavily involved in another team that went by the name of 'Goldthorn FC'. It is recorded that he played in goal for this outfit well into the 1890s.)

Writing on the eve of the FA Cup final in 1908, Brodie remembered how he and Jack Baynton had each captained teams of schoolboys in playground matches. In recalling those days of some thirty years earlier, he mentioned several 'players' who were to be important in the history of the club, including Charlie Mason (Jeremiah's son) and John Addenbroke. Addenbroke was to become the longest serving secretary/manager in Wolves' history, with over thirty-four years of unbroken service.

A very successful football club existed on the other side of Wolverhampton at the time, and Brodie admitted that he and his fellows tried to emulate its deeds and exploits in their games, in true *Boys' Own* style. Captained by Charles Crump, the Great Western Railway engine works on the Stafford Road had a well-established team that had achieved considerable success in FA Cup competitions in the 1870s.

By the summer of 1876, at Fergal Hill's suggestion, fourteen-year-old Brodie and his friend John Baynton had decided to start a team of their own, and canvassed support from old schoolmates. By late autumn their plans were well advanced. They got permission from the vicar (the Revd John Parry) to hold a meeting in the school at 7.30 p.m. on 10 November for 'gentlemen interested' in joining the 'Goldthorn Football Club'. The boys were successful in their new venture, as many keen former pupils still lived in the maze of small streets in and around Blakenhall and retained links with St Luke's by being members of the church choir. Among those who signed up for new team were George Blackburn (later described as a 'gentle centre-half') and the brothers Arthur and George Worall. George Worall was elected as secretary of the new club and John Baynton became the first captain of the team. It was agreed that each player should pay 1s to join the club, and then contribute 1d a week subscription. John Baynton, or 'Jack' as he was more commonly called, also acted as club treasurer and seems to have been a good organiser. His father Samuel had been the tenant of the 96-acre Lodge Farm, which lay just to the south of Goldthorn Hill, and Jack sought his family's permission to use some of their land as a football pitch for the newly formed team. They gave Jack and his friends the go-ahead to use an area close to Goldthorn Hill where an old windmill stood, and so it was in 'Windmill Field' that the first football match of the St Luke's team (the nascent Wolves) was played.

The first recorded matches involving 'the Goldthorn Hill team on their own ground near the Orphanage' took place at 3.30 p.m. on 13 January 1877. Playing Stafford Road engine works' experienced second team, Brodie and his teammates had a sharp introduction to the realities of competitive football. The local press reported the match and recorded that 'from the commencement it was evident that the superior strength of the Stafford Road team must result in an easy victory for them'. Despite the match finishing after the report had to go to press, the final score of 8-0 against Brodie's team reflected how far the old boys from St Luke's would have to progress if they were to compete on a par with other, more established teams from the area.

During the course of the next couple of years, Brodie's young team played games at Lodge Farm on a sporadic basis against other newly formed teams from around the Wolverhampton area. These included Wednesfield Rovers, Red Cross St FC and Wolverhampton Rangers, but very often it was difficult to find teams to play. Brodie described a peculiar encounter with a local rugby club called the 'Crusaders'. Agreeing to a two-leg contest, the St Luke's team played the Crusaders at the Windmill Field and won comfortably. However, the return fixture at the Crusaders' home ground was played in accordance with Rugby Union rules. Even though they 'borrowed' ten of the Crusaders' first-team players, St Luke's were soundly thrashed. It was after this experience that the boys decided to stick to the 'kicking game'!

The nascent Wolves team originally played the game of football in accordance with a set of rules developed in the South Yorkshire town of Sheffield. This code, or 'the Sheffield Rules' as it was generally known, had been devised by Nathaniel Creswick and William Prest specifically for the Sheffield Football Association upon its formation in 1867. The popularity of the code soon spread beyond the borders of Yorkshire, and by the mid-1870s it was the most commonly used set of rules by English football clubs. There were some of the Sheffield Rules that would be recognised by present-day followers of the game (such as a place-kick from the centre spot to start a match and corner kicks), but a great deal that was considered acceptable then would now be seen as foul play. Players were allowed to catch the ball and push their opponents, but not trip or hack at them. Oddly, according to the rules, each player had to provide himself with one red and one blue flannel cap, to be worn by members of a team in a game to distinguish themselves from the opposition (it seems this proviso had been dropped in favour of team shirts by the time the St Luke's team was formed).

Eventually, in the early 1880s the Sheffield Rules were subsumed into nationally agreed Football Association Rules, which by 1886 had become the accepted code for the emerging sport of football throughout Europe. However, some eight of the original Sheffield Rules are still used in football matches throughout the world today.

Within four years of its inception, the St Luke's team had become established on the Wolverhampton football scene, but it was during this time that Jack Baynton's family felt obliged to surrender the tenancy of Lodge Farm. Baynton's widowed mother, Martha, had managed the farm with the help of her older children, but as they reached the age where they married and left home, it had all become too onerous for her. Upon leaving the farm, she was forced to seek work elsewhere in order to support her younger children, and she managed to obtain the position of housekeeper at the Greyhound public house on Lane Green Road in the Staffordshire village of Bilbrook. For the St Luke's team there were serious consequences resulting from the Bayntons giving up the farm. With the change of tenancy at Lodge Farm, the St Luke's boys were forced to find a new venue on which to play matches after only two seasons at the Windmill Field. They were fortunate to be able to rent land very close to St Luke's church in Villiers Street. A field belonging to John Harper (a trader with business interests in the nearby villages of Wednesfield and Willenhall) became their home ground for the next two years, prior to moving to Dudley Road – their third ground – in the summer of 1881.

Alfred Hickman, the team's honorary president, was a keen cricketer and a member of a club that played the game on a field 'on the Dudley Road adjacent to Stroud's factory'. The cricket team were called the 'Wanderers'. Brodie and Baynton had tentatively approached Hickman for support and sponsorship as far back as 1875, and in him they found a loyal friend and supporter. He was no mean sportsman himself, having built one of the first tennis courts in the Wolverhampton area in the grounds of his house. In 1894 Jack Brodie described how the two teenagers had first approached the rich and famous industrialist:

> We passed Mr Hickman's house every day going to practice, and we didn't know what to do for funds. We heard how good he had been to other clubs, and whether it was 'like our cheek and impudence' or not – for we were only boys of about thirteen or fourteen – we wrote to him and asked him to be our president. He accepted and forwarded two guineas.

Alfred Hickman was steadfast in his support for many years and he took a paternalistic overview of the emerging Wolves. He was very aware that his young footballers needed a larger, more secure playing field for their home ground, and he negotiated an amalgamation of St Luke's and the Wanderers. It seemed an ideal solution, as the Dudley Road site had more space and amenities for the footballers' growing band of supporters (e.g. a lean-to sheltered stand) than either Windmill Field or John Harper's Field – although the team used a room at Jeremiah Mason's pub, the King's Arms, over a mile away as its changing room. As seasonal sports (cricket being played in the summer months while the football season occurred during the autumn and winter), there would be no clashes, nor double-booking of the playing area, but the arrangement benefited both in that ground maintenance costs could be shared between the two teams.

Some Wolves historians believe that the St Luke's team adopted the name 'Wanderers' in honour of a very successful London team of the time who went by the same name.

However, Brodie himself wrote that the footballers adopted the title 'Wanderers' at the time of the amalgamation with the cricket team, because the latter insisted. It seems that Jack Brodie and his teammates were very reluctant to ditch their original club name and the link with St Luke's. However, the cricketers 'stoutly maintained that as we were coming to their field, the greater benefit was being conferred upon us'. He went on, 'After considerable discussion we acknowledged the justice of their contention, and henceforth we assumed the name of the Wanderers Football & Cricket Club.'

Brodie's account of the events may not have been as non-contentious and trouble-free as he suggested. A team by the name of St Luke's was still playing in the area some years later, so it may have been that the new Wanderers were effectively a breakaway group from the original church-based team. Little evidence exists to verify if this was indeed the case, but what is known is that the Dudley Road team would go on from success to success, and leave any parish team far behind in its wake. The Wanderers team soon had the prefix 'Wolverhampton' added to their new name, but the players became known to all and sundry as simply 'the Wolves'.

The first season at Dudley Road was very successful for the newly christened Wolves. It was here that Wolves started to play some of the more prominent local teams. Brodie himself recalled the first 'big game' at Dudley Road. Their opponents were Wednesbury Old Athletic and a staggering £6 was taken in gate receipts. However, Jack Brodie was only able to turn out for the team occasionally over the course of the next couple of years. Issues of career development were taking precedence over football playing.

Towards the end of 1880, Jack was facing some important decisions that would affect his long-term future as an educator. He was entering the final phase of his teaching apprenticeship at St Luke's, and he had decided to try and gain admission to Saltley College to gain certified teacher qualifications and status. He was determined to adopt a more dedicated approach to his work, and sought the counsel of Harry Barcroft. On 17 October 1880, the head wrote in the school log, 'I spoke to John Brodie particularly. He promises to do better.' He seems to have kept to his word, and attended extra lessons before school opened each day. Jack's work went from being described as 'unsatisfactory' to 'materially improved' in a four-month period in the spring of 1880. A key factor in Brodie's improved performance may have been that his old 'partner in crime', Jack Baynton, left the school and moved to Birmingham for a short while at Easter that year, leaving little to distract Jack Brodie from his studies.

As the year went on, Brodie's overall ratings continued to improve. With Baynton having departed, Jack became the senior pupil-teacher at St Luke's and took on a mentoring role to the younger apprentice teachers, including John Addenbrooke.

By the beginning of July 1881, Jack Brodie was concentrating on preparing for the Saltey Entrance Examination and was granted a leave of absence for 'private study' by Harry Barcroft and the governors of St Luke's. One way or the other, they were all aware that his time as a pupil-teacher at the school was coming to an end. Harry Barcroft selected a young monitor called Walters to 'work up to take John Brodie's place at the end of the school year'.

On a Saturday morning in mid-July 1881, eighteen-year-old Brodie caught a local train to Birmingham. He was off to St Peter's Teacher Training College at Saltley, where he would sit the annually held entrance examination. Saltley College, an all-male Anglican foundation, had been built by Charles Bowyer Adderley and opened in 1852. Originally, St Peter's College catered for thirty students, but by the time Brodie sought admission it had expanded to take in forty-six trainee teachers every year. The governors of St Peter's offered places to the best applicants based upon their performance in the entrance exam. The assessment of candidates was based upon their ability in mathematics, literacy and a basic understanding of science. Neatness and clarity of handwriting were also considered important, but the key factor in gaining admission was the applicant's understanding and knowledge of Holy Scripture. John Brodie passed the exam, but with a performance well below the average. He was thirty-third out of the forty-six young men who succeeded in gaining admittance to St Peter's and was described as a 'third-class scholar'. Training to be a teacher in Victorian times at Saltley was not cheap. The fee for the entrance exam alone was £5, and invariably students would need the support of a sponsor. With good reports from Harry Barcroft and the vicar of St Luke's, John Brodie had merited the support of the Dioceses of Lichfield, which not only reimbursed £4 10s of the exam fee, but also gave him a subsistence grant of £15 while he trained. This covered Brodie's 'board, lodging, washing and medical attendance' while at St Peter's, but his scholarship also depended upon the 'good conduct and diligence of the holder and fitness for the office of teacher'. College principal, the Revd Frederick Burridge MA, made it clearly understood from the outset that poor conduct by students would not be accepted, and that parents and friends would be legally liable to maintain any student who was suspended by the college for any reason. However, such issues were not a concern of young John Brodie. He was going to Saltley to work hard and qualify in his chosen trade. On 4 February 1881, Harry Barcroft wrote in the school log, 'John Brodie attended school for the last time on Monday morning.'

During the course of the next year and a half, Brodie learnt a great deal and made good progress. In his first year at St Peter's he gained a certificate for drawing and was judged 'to play the harmonium good enough for Church services'. He also passed the religious education exam held in October 1881, and gained Class II Honours in the science exam held two months later. Jack seems to have been particularly good at science, as he passed a further exam in 'animal physiology, sound, light and heat' a year later.

Life at Saltley was not all about undertaking and passing exams. It was quite a spartan existence, but Jack Brodie enjoyed a full social life with his new college mates. As well as geology and history excursions to nearby Worcestershire, there were clubs (such as astronomy) and a debating society for students. Formal dinners and variety and music concerts in which students participated were held on a regular basis. However, with so many young men on site, it is not surprising that sport played an important part in life of St Peter's College and Jack Brodie involved himself to the full. If they so wished, students could use the college rifle range, but both cricket and football were more generally more popular. Brodie played for the college football team in both his first and second year, during which time they reached the latter stages of the Birmingham Cup (a competition for local teams only second in importance to the nationally contested FA Cup). The quality of the Saltley College team can be gauged by the fact that it was one of the founding members of the Birmingham branch of the Football Association and had a well-established reputation well before many other more famous local football clubs. For example, in 1875 the Small Heath Alliance (later known as Birmingham City FC) played its first game against the students of Saltley College. Interestingly, in his second year at Saltley, Brodie captained the college team against a visiting Wolves XI in a friendly match. This seems to be the only recorded instance of Jack Brodie turning out in a competitive game against the team he had helped to found.

It is no surprise that football flourished at Saltley, as Frederick Burridge had done much to ensure that it was played regularly on an organised basis. Football in Britain has benefited from his foresight, as not only did student John Brodie (and later John Addenbrooke) go on to help consolidate Wolverhampton Wanderers as a major force in the national game, but other Saltley old boys helped set up famous clubs such as Derby County and Stoke City.

At the end of the autumn term 1882, Jack Brodie left St Peter's College and returned to Wolverhampton. He was now a fully qualified and certificated assistant teacher, but he was unable to find a suitable post straight away, and undertook short-term, temporary work at a various church schools, such as St Luke's and St John's. It was not until the 21 May 1883 that he was able to take up a permanent post in the boys' department at St Peter's elementary school, which was situated in the town centre. The post had become vacant due to a teacher called Harrison leaving to work in a school in Short Heath in Willenhall. Described in the school logbook as an 'Assistant Master Second Class', Brodie stayed at the school for a little over four years, but spent his time away from the classroom turning out for the Wolves.

The 1880s was perhaps the most important decade in the history of Wolverhampton Wanderers, for it was during those ten years that it went from being little more than a gang of mates having a kick-about to a cup finalist team, and became perceived as a football club of national importance. The improvement and development of the club during this time mirrors the most fertile and productive of John Brodie's career as a footballer.

Upon leaving college, Jack Brodie had not only returned to his home town, but also the football club that was so dear to his heart. The football season for Wolves had started on 1 October 1881, with the opening game at Dudley Road being played against Stourbridge Standard. Jack Baynton had captained the side with 'nearly 200 people assembled to witness the match'. Wanderers ran out eventual 7-1 winners.

Wanderers were lucky at the time to have gained the interest and assistance of Macclesfield-born Levi 'Dough' Johnson. Johnson was the landlord of a public house on the Dudley Road called the Ring o' Bells, and a close friend of Jeremiah Mason. Mason encouraged Johnson to become the treasurer to the St Luke's team in late 1870s, when gates had been low and money scarce. His efforts resulted in the club making a profit of £5 6s 7½d in their first year at Dudley Road. The success was to continue, as the following year Wolves declared that £80 had been taken in gate receipts!

The 1881/82 season was one of consolidation for the new Wolves. It was during this time that the people of Wolverhampton started to become aware of the potential of the Wanderers, and a small but loyal group of supporters started to follow the team on a regular basis. The team colours of faded red (sometimes described as a 'dirty pink') and white-striped shirts and dark-blue shorts (known as 'knickers' at the time) became the official and established team kit. Brodie himself was only available for team selection after the Christmas holiday, when he had come down from Saltley College.

The following season witnessed the first the major setback for the young Wolves team. Thomas Blackham was a former classmate and neighbour of Jack Brodie from the time he had been living in Haggar Street. Known to everyone as 'Arthur', Blackham was a founder member of the St Luke's team and had played regularly over the previous five years. After having scored in a game against Villa Cross on Christmas Eve 1883, Blackham was unfortunate enough to break his leg. Obviously this marred the magnificent 15-0 scoreline, especially as the injury was so serious that that Blackham was forced to retire completely from playing. However, he maintained strong links with the club and served as both a committee member and linesman for many years.

Despite this and one or two other setbacks, on the whole Wolves started to go from strength to strength. The committee appointed the team's first recognised trainer. This was William Shipton, who was the landlord of a public house called the Vine that was located in the Upper Vauxhall area off the Tettenhall Road. Shipton's training methods were rather simplistic and seem far from demanding on Brodie and his fellow players. He organised long healthy walks in the countryside around Wolverhampton and it is reported that the whole team actually strolled as far as Penkridge on one occasion. Dietary concerns do not seem to have played a part in Shipton's approach to player fitness, as it was reported that team members looked forward to their post-match meals of pork chops and eggs at Levi Johnson's Ring 'o Bells on the Dudley Road.

Important things were happening on the field of play as well during this season. Wolves entered the Football Association Cup competition for first time. Their first game in what was to be a century and a quarter's involvement in the competition took place against Long Eaton Rangers on 27 October 1883. Wolves went 1-0 down, and Brodie's goal in the first half was declared illegal by the umpire (later to be retitled 'referee'), Henry Dallard. The action of Dallard (a founder of Walsall Swifts in 1874) seem to have spurred Jack Brodie on to greater efforts. He managed to score Wolves' second goal on sixty-six minutes and his second on seventy-four minutes. Wolves won 4-1. Despite Jack Brodie's heroics in this game, having the honour of scoring Wolves' first-ever FA Cup goal, the club's progress in the competition was short-lived. They subsequently went down 4-2 to Wednesbury Old Athletic (whom Brodie described as the 'crack team of the area') in the second round. Brodie scored both of the Wolves' goals in that game.

Despite the disappointment of being dumped out of the FA Cup competition, the season was far from being a washout, as Wolves lifted their first trophy in the spring of 1884. For the second year running, they had entered the Wrekin Cup competition. Although this was essentially a regional competition, several big-name teams had entered. Participation in the Wrekin Cup during the 1883/84 season helped to confirm Wolves as the main team from Wolverhampton, when at the second time of asking they beat their old adversaries, Stafford Roaders, in the process of reaching the final. In the course of the Wrekin Cup competition, Brodie's Wolves played five matches, scoring twenty-nine goals and conceding none. In the final against Hadley, Wolves ran out the eventual winners 11-0. Brodie recalled returning to the centre of the pitch and, looking back at Wolves' goalkeeper, he 'nearly collapsed with laughter'. Isaac Giffiths, (known as 'Little Ike') was so bored with the lack of activity from the Hadley forwards that he was 'calmly seated on the crossbar, where he had climbed to obtain a better view of proceedings'.

Brodie scored six goals in the final, and the trophy still has pride of place in the Wolves' cabinets. Nowadays it is the Wolves Charity Cup and it is competed for by local teams on an annual basis.

With their first silverware secure in the trophy cabinet, Wolves could be proud of their achievements that year, but they were to suffer another setback when Jack Brodie's old friend Jimmy Hill was forced to leave the team after suffering a serious knee injury. Failing to find suitable employment locally, Hill moved to London and got a job at Woolwich Arsenal. There he continued his interest in football and, along with Bob Critchton, helped to found and develop the world-famous Arsenal Football Club, the 'Gunners'.

Returning to the Wolves, the 1884/85 season seems to have been something of an anticlimax after the great excitement of winning a trophy the previous year. The Wanderers were beaten two goals to four in round one the FA Cup competition by a team from Derby (interestingly also called St Luke's). Brodie was responsible for one of the Wanderers' goals. However, despite disappointment on the field of play, the quality of Wolves' support and organisational structure was improving greatly. The club was very fortunate to have a local businessman named Charles Forder join the committee to supplement the organisational and financial acumen of Levi Johnson and Alfred Hickman. Forder had made his wealth from the manufacture of hansom cabs in his workshops on the Bilston Road, directly opposite the town's Royal Hospital. The organisational aspect of the club's structure was fairly well completed a year later when in August 1885 one of the original St Luke's Football Club members, and more lately a Wolves reserve player, Jack Addenbrooke, became the club's first paid official, appointed into a combined role of secretary and team manager.

The ensuing season saw Wolverhampton Wanderers exact a savage revenge on Derby St Luke's in the FA Cup of that year. On 31 October the two teams met in what turned out to be a very uneven contest, with Wolves running out winners by seven goals to none conceded. Jack Brodie scored two in this match and another in Wolves' 2-1 third-round win over Walsall on 12 December. Sadly, Brodie and his teammates' luck in the FA Cup did not last much into the new year of 1885, when they went down 1-3 to West Bromwich Albion in January.

The following years saw Wolves acquire players who were to become some of the most famous in the early history of the club. Twenty-year-old Harry Allen was signed from Walsall Swifts in the summer of 1886. He had played for his home-town club for three years before coming to the Dudley Road outfit, but he soon became a firm favourite with the sons of Wulfruna. Allen was a centre-half, a man of massive stature whose presence on the pitch filled Brodie with awe. Like Brodie, Harry Allen was to become one of Wolves' greatest players and went on to represent his country, earning five full caps for England. He was to retire through injury in October 1894, and after short spells running a public house in Wolverhampton and working as a coalman, he died just one year later aged twenty-nine.

The next year, Wolves continued to strengthen the side with further inspired signings. Wolverhampton-born Albert Fletcher joined his home-town team from Willenhall Pickwick. Fletcher's signature was finally secured when he accepted a golden guinea from Wolves' secretary Jack Addenbrooke. Although he took a while to get into the first team, Albert Fletcher eventually became a fixture in the Wolves squad. Playing in defence or midfield, Fletcher's skill was eventually recognised by the national team selectors. He was awarded the first of two full England caps in the 1888/89 season when he combined with teammate Arthur Lowder to form one of the most formidable half-back lines in the country. Although Albert Fletcher's playing career was cut short when he suffered a broken leg in a game against Aston Villa in March 1891, he continued to be an important part of the Wolves' setup for many years. He became the team's 'sponge man' and eventually the first-team trainer. He was to hold this position for almost a quarter of a century until his retirement in 1920.

Around the same time that Fletcher became part of the Wolves team, the club were fortunate to sign Richard Baugh. Known by everyone as 'Dick', Baugh was the son of a coal miner and had been born in Chesterfield in 1864. He had attended St Luke's School along with Jack Brodie in the 1870s and had played for a variety of local sides, including Rose Villa and Wolverhampton Rangers. Dick Baugh had been one of the leading lights of the Great Western engine works, but jumped at the chance of joining Wolves when the 'Roaders' started to decline. As a hard tackling and thoughtful full-back, Baugh was to play for Wolves in over 220 matches in the ten years between 1886 and 1896. He appeared in three cup finals and was awarded two full England caps, although he only scored once for Wolves. He left the club in the summer of 1896, although his son (also called 'Dickie' Baugh) was to play for the Wanderers in the years after the First World War had ended.

The rapid growth in the popularity of football in Wolverhampton during the first half of the 1880s meant that the Wolves had become quite a significant business in the town. Although the Wolves recorded a turnover of over a thousand pounds for the 1886/87 season, the club was not in a healthy financial position. News of such problems off the field quickly spread amongst the townsfolk of Wolverhampton, but worse news was to follow: Jack Brodie announced his retirement from football.

Wolves played four epic FA Cup games against Aston Villa in the spring of 1887, prior to the Birmingham team finally taking the tie by an odd goal. The competiveness of the matches took their toll and Jack Brodie suffered a severe injury in the first replay. Just short of his twenty-sixth birthday, he decided that he'd had enough.

At the annual club dinner, held on 8 August at the Coach & Horses Hotel on Snowhill, Alfred Hickman summed up the season for the audience:

> They [Wolves] had won forty-one and only lost fourteen (cheers). He went on by referring directly to the cup matches. In the contest for the English Cup they had fought for three long days (hear, hear) – three undecided days – bravely, sternly and well (hear, hear) – and on the fourth day they lost (laughter). He did not laugh. He felt grieved, especially as he knew it was not fairly lost (hear, hear). It was lost because their gallant captain (Brodie) was disabled (loud cheers). They all knew very well except for that accident in all human possibility they must have either tied or won (hear, hear).

Hickman employed some fine Victorian rhetoric to describe the importance of Wolves in Britain's emerging national game and what made a great player like Jack Brodie:

> The Wanderers Football Club was second to none (hear, hear). Football was not mere play. The good influence that the game carried far and wide were not evident perhaps on the surface, and not until they began to think. Only the English nation and her colonies could produce a club like theirs (hear, hear). The same qualities that made a football player were the same that

carried the English flag triumphantly ('hear, hear' and cheers). Among those qualities were stern discipline, resource under difficulties and courage (hear, hear). He believed that during their last season their football playing had been witnessed by over 200,000 spectators. That was a great statement and he did not believe that one of those spectators went away without being the better for the sight they saw (hear, hear). They saw a splendid exhibition of manly qualities (hear, hear) and it was impossible that they could have gone away without feeling, at any rate, to some extent, inclined to emulate what they had seen. Pointedly, he stated they should all 'strive to be a Brodie'.

Members the town council also expressed their appreciation of Brodie's significance to Wolverhampton Wanderers, but the most significant comments came from Charles Crump, by now president of the Birmingham FA. He surprised the audience by saying that John Brodie has not been a good captain. He quickly added that this was because he was 'too fair to his opponents'.

In his response Jack Brodie picked up on this issue and stated that 'he would rather lose a game fairly than win it by unfair means'. He explained his reasons for leaving the Wolves. He said, 'No one was more grieved over giving up active participation in the game of football than himself, but he felt the time had come when he must leave the field ('no, no') and give it up, He had other things to think about. It was all very well to have a game at football, but it should not be placed before business, or what was to get their daily bread (hear, hear).' In conclusion he attempted to put his contribution to the Wolves team in perspective: 'He hoped his giving up the game would not be a loss to the club. There was as good fish in the sea, as those which had been caught, but they required catching.'

Apart from his injury, there were other reasons Jack Brodie was becoming less concerned with football. Changes in his domestic circumstances had altered his priorities. He had recently got married to a local girl and his father was becoming increasingly unwell, which was affecting Jack greatly. These growing family responsibilities, along with commitment to his teaching career, meant he was not willing nor able to give as much time to playing for Wolves as he had been.

Some ten years before, when Jack Brodie had been busy learning his trade in the boys' department at St Luke's, a young girl named Eda Lockley had been taken on as a pupil-teacher at the infant school. Eda (or Ada as she was sometimes known) was three years younger than Jack, but they had much in common. Like Brodie's grandfather, Eda's father Charles Lockley was a blacksmith by trade, but in the 1870s he was working for a wealthy 'master locksmith' called James Hodge. Hodge employed seventeen men and apprentices at his workshops on Goldthorn Hill, known locally as 'Hodge's Buildings'. Eda and her family lived in accommodation at Hodge's workshops, and like Jack Brodie she had been educated at St Luke's before returning to the school as a trainee teacher. Eda had to work hard in her role as pupil-teacher, but was subject to criticism by the mistress in charge of the infant and girls' department at St Luke's. On 26 June 1876 the teacher overseeing Eda's training felt she 'was compelled to give the pupil-teacher a severe reproof for negligence in the home lessons'. However, she must have heeded such warnings and improved her performance in the classroom, as it was reported on 12 March 1880 that Eda Lockley had 'passed fairly' an examination of her abilities as an elementary teacher.

She later gained a First Class Pass in the 'Examination for the Queen's Scholarship in Teaching'. The result of this success was that St Luke's was awarded a 60s (£3) prize for training Eda so well.

So, although she did not go on to teacher training college as Jack did, Eda earned her certificate as a qualified teacher by undertaking her duties as a pupil-teacher for five years at St Luke's. By the time she qualified in the early 1880s, Eda had gained experience both as an infants' teacher and in the older girls' department of the school. In 1887, while he was teaching at St Peter's, Jack married Eda at St Luke's on the 9 April. They were to be happily wed for only fifteen years before Eda tragically died from tuberculosis in December 1902. When she passed away in his arms at the age of only thirty-eight years, a heartbroken Jack was left to bring up their family of John, aged twelve, Harold, eight, and their little four-year-old daughter Phyllis. All three children had 'Lockley' as their middle names in memory of Eda's maiden name.

The season following Jack Brodie's departure from the club was not a good one for Wolves. In the three FA Cup matches that took place during the winter and spring months, Wolves only found their opponents' net on five occasions (and one of those was an own goal). Brodie's playing skills and abilities were certainly being missed. However, even without his massive contribution, Wolverhampton Wanderers were still developing their resources. Under Levi Johnson's financial leadership, improvements were made to the Dudley Road ground in the summer of 1887. Ironwork barriers were put in place to increase crowd safety and supporters' comfort was addressed by the erection of a lean-to shelter to protect them from the elements. Investors had been encouraged to finance a 'refreshment tent' (oddly enough constructed of corrugated metal) and changing rooms christened 'the Pavilion'. It seemed Wolves would be at Dudley Road for many years to come, but events behind the scenes would change all that.

Despite the investment and careful thrift of the Wanderers' treasurer, the club's finances had become perilous. In spite of having a turnover in excess of £1,000 a season, a great deal of the money went to servicing debt. Also, the club had a reserve team that was bringing in gate receipts less than half the cost of its running. What had started as a football club of amateur players had become quite a large commercial concern in little over a decade. It is unlikely those involved with the original team could have foreseen the financial and organisational implications of Wolverhampton Wanderers' rapid growth during its first few years.

Discussions took place regarding disbanding the reserves and even abandoning weekly training sessions for the first XI. It was felt by some of the club committee that the team was not as well supported by local people compared with the likes of West Bromwich Albion and Aston Villa, both of whom had annual incomes at least twice that of Wolves. A new chairman was appointed at Wolves. He was a thirty-five-year-old pork butcher and town councillor named Arthur Hollingsworth. Hollingsworth had big plans for the Wolves, which events happening elsewhere were helping to form.

The established football clubs of the period all faced the same problem. The demand to see football matches had grown considerably during the late 1870s and the 1880s, but once a team had been eliminated from the FA Cup or local trophy competitions, there was really nothing to play for. It was hard to maintain popular interest and support by playing friendly matches alone. In 1887, a Scotsman named William McGregor, who was a director of Aston Villa, was concerned about what he saw as the chaotic practice of clubs arranging their own fixtures and set about rectifying this. Inspired by an account of a proposal to introduce a league system to American college football that appeared in the British press in 1887, he invited twelve established clubs (including Wolves and neighbours West Bromwich Albion) to form a 'Football League'. Utilising the English railway network, it was envisaged that teams would visit and play each other both home and away over the course of a playing season for the right to be called 'champions'! It would coexist with the existing FA Cup competition, which would mean that there were a lot more regular football matches to be played over the course of a season, by which supporters' excitement and interest could be maintained. The effect of the introduction of League football in 1888 was that there was a surge in interest and support for the game throughout the country.

The growth in interest in the game around this time can be attested to by an interesting case that appeared before Wolverhampton magistrates in October 1888. Three local boys named Frederick Shaw, aged thirteen, George Finnemore, also aged thirteen, and eleven-year-old Edward Evans, were jointly charged with stealing six silk handkerchiefs from a market stallholder named Samuel Cutts. The handkerchiefs were valued at 11s, and it was said the boys had intended to sell them and buy a ball with the proceeds as 'they had become infatuated with football'! The parents of the young miscreants told the Bench that they had already punished their sons for thieving, but after warning the lads about their future conduct the magistrates bound the parents over for three months to ensure they controlled the boys better.

Wolves started their first League programme with a credible 1-1 draw against Aston Villa, at a game played on 8 September 1888 at Dudley Road in front of 2,000 spectators (Wolves' first League goal came courtesy of Villa's Cox putting the ball into his own net). Over the next couple of months, Wolves had a succession of draws and a couple of wins, but on 20 October that year great excitement must have gone around the Wolves supporters who had travelled to Blackburn to watch their team play their seventh game of the campaign against Rovers. A familiar figure strode onto the field of play and took his rightful position on the Wolves forward line. Jack Brodie was back.

It is unclear why Jack Brodie came out of his self-imposed retirement to lead his beloved Wolves once again. It is certainly true that his decision to play again was influenced by the surge in popular enthusiasm for football that accompanied the birth of the League, but changes in his personal circumstances had perhaps also helped him come to his decision. Not playing for well over a year meant that he had fully recovered from his knee injury, and his teaching career had entered a new phase when, in the previous November, he had been appointed to the headship of Brewood National School, while his wife took control of the infants' department. Moving to Brewood for positions of great responsibility and taking up residence in the spacious 'master's house' adjacent to the school might have been taxing enough for Jack and Eda, but adding to their workload was the fact that Eda gave birth to their first child (John Lockley Brodie) in June 1888. Although now a man of considerable local status, a father and a loving husband, it might well have been that Jack Brodie would have wanted to return to the Wanderers at the start of the 1888 season, but he did not actually play until some two months later. His wife had become extremely ill in the middle of that year, so much so that part of the school had to close because she was unable to teach the children. (After this time, Eda Brodie suffered a great deal of illness. In 1891 she was away from school for a full two months and finally in the following year resigned altogether due to her continuous ill health.)

Whatever the speculation as to Jack Brodie's reasons for taking up 'the beautiful game' again, what *is* certain is that his return had a dramatic effect on Wolves' fortunes.

Not only did Brodie score in the 2-2 draw that day against Blackburn, he went on to successfully find the net in the next eight games on the trot. A Wolves player did not match this remarkable feat for another thirty-seven years, when Tom Phillipson scored thirteen goals in ten consecutive matches for the Wanderers.

Jack Brodie's magnificent scoring record and his renewed enthusiasm for the game had not gone unnoticed in the corridors of power at FA headquarters in London. In the spring of 1889, Brodie was called up into the England international XI to play against Ireland at Everton's Goodison Park. He was the 146th player to pull on the white shirt of England and scored a goal in what became a 6-0 drubbing of the men 'from over the water'. (He received a second international cap against Scotland at the Oval some months later, but sadly failed to score as the Scots ran out eventual winners.)

Not only did Brodie's goals help Wolverhampton Wanderers achieve third spot in the first annual Football League rankings, but they also reached their first-ever FA Cup final in 1889. In getting to the final, Wolves had scored sixteen goals to five against (Brodie had scored one), and they met Preston North End in the final at the Oval in London on 30 March 1889.

The Preston team of the time was the most successful the game had ever known, and Wolves knew they would have their work cut out to beat the famous 'Invincibles'. Playing in front of a crowd of 22,500, Brodie led the team out for the biggest match of the club's history. Appearing in front of the largest-ever crowd to watch the Wolves play up until that time, the men from the Midlands were given little chance of winning – and the pundits were not wrong! Major Francis Marindin, the president of the FA, took charge of the match, and the linesmen were J. C. Clegg and Lord Kinnaird. The kick-off had been delayed until 4 p.m. to ensure the event did not clash with the then much more prestigious University Boat Race, which took place that afternoon. Despite hitting the crossbar early on in the game, Wolves were to have few chances and seemed to be overwhelmed by the occasion. Brodie recalled the game through rose-tinted spectacles some twenty years later. In 1908 he wrote:

> The match was memorable by reason of the utter absence of any reward for the Wanderers' efforts. For fully twenty minutes they rained in shot, but the Preston goalkeeper the celebrated Mills-Roberts gave one of the most magnificent exhibitions I have ever witnessed.

Few agreed with his analysis. Most believed Wolves were well outplayed and the 3-0 goal tally was a true reflection of each team's prowess on the day. As the *Daily News* stated in its report on the game, 'Judged by their play on Saturday, the Wolverhampton Wanderers have still a great deal to learn before they can expect to cope successfully with Preston North End.'

Jack Brodie himself did not have a good game, as his mind was elsewhere. Shortly before the final in the spring of 1889, his father Henry Brodie died aged around fifty years, after a long illness. The worry of his father's decline had affected Jack Brodie, and he lost over two stone in weight. The Wolves team wore black armbands as an act of sympathy and solidarity with Jack Brodie during the game following Henry Brodie's death.

After the game, club president Alfred Hickman held a dinner at London's Constitutional Club (Hickman had failed to see the game as his horse-drawn carriage had been involved in an accident on the way to the Oval in which he suffered some slight injuries). Speaking at the dinner, Jack Brodie said of the Wolves 'for eleven years it had been a hard, uphill fight, but he was very proud in having at length brought his team to the Oval (cheers). They must hope for success another year (hear, hear).'

Twenty years later, Jack Brodie restated the magnitude of the club's achievement in 1889. In spite of all their difficulties, reaching the national FA final at all showed how far Wolverhampton Wanderers had come in that time. He described (rather inaccurately) that getting to the final had been 'a grand achievement for eleven men born within 6 miles of the ground'.

At the end of this remarkable season for Brodie and his team, Hollingsworth, the new chairman of Wolverhampton Wanderers, started making plans for the club's future. Opposite his home on Waterloo Road, on the northern side of Wolverhampton's town centre, lay the Molineux Grounds. Originally the private gardens for the Molineux family, who lived in the large house that still bears their name, the land had been put to many different uses during the mid-nineteenth century, including being a pleasure park, town exhibition centre and a skating rink. In more recent times it had gained fame as a cycling track and lately as a sports ground. In the 1888/89 season the Stafford Road team had played their matches there after leaving their traditional Fox Lane venue, but it was a club in decline and there were no plans for them to continue playing at Molineux Grounds in the future. An enterprising brewery from the East Midlands had bought Molineux House with a view to running it as a hotel, but saw great potential profits if a thriving, well-supported football club could be encouraged to take the grounds and make it their 'home' venue. Wolverhampton Wanderers, riding on the crest of a wave at the time, clearly fitted the bill. Northampton Brewery made approaches to Hollingsworth, who saw great merit in their proposal for Wolves to move to the Molineux, but he knew he would have to plan carefully if the proposal was ever to be realised.

The annual general meeting of the Wolverhampton Wanderers club for the 1888/89 season took place on the evening of Friday 7 June 1889 at the Assembly Rooms of the Exchange Building in the town. The meeting was presided over by a committee member named Rhodes (a convention that allowed Hollingsworth to address the meeting from the floor and make proposals). Rather surprisingly, club president Alfred Hickman was not present at the gathering, although the meeting started with a telegram from him being read to the meeting by Rhodes. In the telegram Hickman expressed his regret at not being at the meeting due to being in London on business, but added rather pointedly, 'I wish I had known of your meeting sooner.' This suggests that the meeting had been put together rather quickly, which seems a little odd considering it was the regular annual meeting and its date would have been known a long time in advance. (The implication of Hickman's absence was that his considerable influence could not be brought to bear in any important decisions that might be made at the meeting.) The club's finances were discussed and the balance sheet for the season was read out. Despite a turnover of £1,740 17s 9d, Wolves were in serious debt. Cost-cutting measures were openly discussed, such as disbanding the reserve team and even abandoning team-training sessions, which it was claimed was costing £291 19s 7½d.

W. H. Jope (a member of the Football Association Council) addressed the meeting and set the scene for ensuing events. He said that although Wolves attracted good crowds away from home, there was a problem with the size of home gates, as the receipts showed. Pointedly, he posed the question, 'Would an improvement be effected by having a ground nearer to the town, (hear, hear), and more convenient to the public?' He reinforced the point by adding, 'Was it possible by a little capital outlay to get a more sheltered and attractive field?' Hollingsworth stated that getting to the final of the FA Cup had actually cost the club over £40, and the loss on staging League games had been £130. Clearly such losses could not continue, and Hollingsworth rammed home his point that the Dudley Road ground would need to have between £150 and £200 spent on it in the forthcoming season. He then told the meeting that he had agreed with Northampton Brewery that Wolves should take the Molineux Grounds at an annual rent of £50, subject to confirmation. Hoping to appease potential opposition to the move, Hollingsworth then paid a glowing tribute to the club treasurer, Levi Johnson, 'who had nursed the club in its infancy'. Hollingsworth then proposed the motion 'that this meeting cordially supports the action of the committee in reference to the taking of Molineux Grounds'.

It seems that the club chairman's flattering words had cut little ice with Levi Johnson, who 'complained very strongly indeed upon the fact that such a drastic change had been sprung upon the meeting'. He believed the issue was a matter of life or death to the club, and that it was 'most improper it should be covered up in the way it had been'. Johnson stoutly tried to defend Wanderers staying at Dudley Road and stated that after subletting the land (for grazing) the annual rent only equated to £9 per year. He added that the Pavilion at Dudley Road had been financed by interest-free loans given by well-wishers, and the unpublicised proposed move was 'an injustice being done to them'. His greatest complaint, however, was that the move away from the Goldthorn area was also a great injustice to the area that had produced such players as Mason, Brodie, Lowder and Baugh. He proposed that the meeting should be suspended for a week while the matter of the move to Molineux was considered, but Hollingsworth had done his 'behind the chair' canvassing well and Johnson's proposal was easily defeated. Hollingsworth's original proposal was passed with loud cheering, with only a Mr Finn voting against. Brodie and the Wolves were moving to the Molineux.

Faced with a *fait accompli,* both Johnson and Alfred Hickman had little choice but to accept the club's move to the Molineux, but it seems that Jack Brodie was pleased with the new venue. He described it as 'one of the finest natural amphitheatres in the British Isles', although it was far from ready when the 1889/90 season kicked off on 7 September. On that Saturday afternoon, the first spectators who entered the ground to watch Wolves play Villa had to pass fallen trees that had only been felled by workmen that morning. Wolves drew the match 1-1, but it wasn't Brodie who scored the first goal at Molineux for Wanderers; that honour went to David Wykes. Described by Jack Brodie as 'rollicking', David Wykes was a popular forward, 'whose ambition was to be an international'. Sadly, this ambition was never realised as the Walsall-born Wykes died suddenly in October 1895, after seven seasons with Wolves.

Brodie himself did not turn out for Wolves until 5 October, when he scored in the home League fixture against Accrington Stanley. On 22 February Brodie gained the distinction of getting the first hat-trick scored by a Wanderers player at Molineux. The match was a cup replay against Stoke, after the FA had declared the first game void following a complaint, and in fact Brodie scored five goals in all that day. He completed the season with a final total of thirteen League and cup goals to his name.

The move to Molineux seems to have been an unqualified success for the club. The first season there saw average League gates rise by almost 20 per cent, but much of this can be put down by the massive 19,000 who turned up on Boxing Day 1889 to see Wolves take on Blackburn Rovers. However, the team's local popularity and following gradually increased, and in time Molineux became synonymous with the Wolves.

During this time finances were always a major concern for the Wolves committee, but it could not be said that great amounts were being spent on players' wages. The club secretary (John Addenbrooke) kept a detailed account of money being paid to the team. Charlie Mason (a semi-professional full-back who had been the first Wolves player to be selected for England) received 10s a game for the first half of the season, and a total of £35 for the season as a whole. The four amateurs on the books (including Jack Brodie) were only paid expenses. He only got 4s 6d in all for the period up to Christmas, and a mere £6 7s 6d for the season in total. Even taking into account the relative purchasing power of money in those times, the amounts Brodie received does not seem a good level of remuneration for such a key member of the Wanderers' setup.

The following season 1890/91 was Jack Brodie's last in Wolves' colours, which had now changed from the light red and white of the St Luke's days to the more recognisable gold and black of today. The change had been effected in honour of Wolverhampton being granted borough status and the town council having adopted the inspirational motto 'out of darkness cometh light'. The Wolves' new colours reflected this. Brodie's first game was on 27 September, when he scored in the 3-2 win over Blackburn. His goal tally continued through the autumn of that season, scoring two against Derby on 11 October. However, the rich source of goals for Wolves that Brodie represented was soon to dry up, and he found the net for a final time on 27 December in a home match against Sunderland. Although this was Jack Brodie's last game for Wolves as a centre-forward, he continued to turn out for his team and even went on to win a third and final international cap. In his final few days as a player, Jack Brodie was honoured by being named captain of an England XI in the first ever international football match to be held at Molineux. Under his leadership, England beat the Irish by six goals to one in front of a crowd of 15,231.

This was the pinnacle of his playing career, but just one week later Jack Brodie played his last competitive football match in a 2-6 defeat against Aston Villa 14 March. He was twenty-nine years of age and was suffering with a recurring problem with his knee, which left him with a limp for the remainder of his life.

There would be no second comeback for Jack Brodie. In all he had played sixty-five official FA Cup and Football League games for Wolves and amassed a tally of forty-four goals. In the cup alone he had scored twenty-two goals in twenty-three appearances. He had won three international caps and was the first Wolves player to score for his country.

Wolves had been a very important part of his life, and Jack Brodie looked back on his years with fondness. He recalled a number of vivid experiences from the Wolves' formative years. He noted that on several occasions at away fixtures, he and his fellow players were forced to change into their playing kit behind a wall or a hedge – not the way a respectable Victorian schoolmaster would normally appear. Despite no longer playing, it did not mean Jack was finished with what was fast becoming the 'national sport'. He was to give the game the benefit of his vast experience and knowledge by becoming a FA referee (a position he was to hold for sixteen years). The first game that Jack Brodie took charge of as a referee was a pre-season practice game between Wolves' first XI and the club's reserves. This game took place in the summer after he had stopped playing, and it is interesting to speculate about whether the Wolves players who knew Jack so well and had lined up alongside him only a few months earlier took him fully seriously in his first game in charge. However, he went on to establish a good reputation as a knowledgeable and scrupulously fair interpreter of 'the rules of the game'. Jack Brodie became a well-known figure at local matches, and indeed was one of the founders of the Wolverhampton Referees' Association in 1910. However, he had also refereed at the highest level, and it is recorded that in 1902 he took charge of a League match between Arsenal and Bristol City. A few years before, in 1895, Jack had refereed another match involving Arsenal. At the Londoners' ground of Manor Field, Brodie was officiating in a Second Division match between the Gunners and Burton Wanderers. A group of Arsenal fans questioned Brodie's impartiality, especially as their opponents were from the same county as the referee. He was assaulted and suffered a broken cheekbone. For their supporters' violent actions, the Arsenal club was punished by the FA, who ordered their ground closed for six weeks.

Brodie continued to serve his old club for a number of years after he had hung his boots up by heading the 'player selection committee'. The task, which is now the sole preserve of a club manager, proved difficult at times. After a particularly poor start to one season where Wolves lost a number of games on the trot, Brodie offered his resignation. However, the directors understood his overall importance and contribution to the club and refused to accept the resignation letter.

Despite his ongoing love affair with football, it was teaching that was at the heart of Jack Brodie's life. During the time of Brodie's first retirement from the game on 18 November 1887, the headmaster of St Peter's in Wolverhampton wrote in his logbook, 'J. Brodie has sent in his resignation having obtained the headmastership at Brewood.'

The village of Brewood in the late nineteenth century was a well-established and thriving agricultural community. The Shropshire Union Canal ran through the village but there was no direct railway link to Wolverhampton and the Black Country, although there was a small station at Four Ashes, just a couple of miles away. A traveller who wished to go directly to Wolverhampton from Brewood had to rely on the thrice-weekly private horse-drawn cab service or rent a horse. As the new headmaster of the village school, John Brodie was able to afford his own pony and trap in order to travel around the village and to the railway station for journeys further afield. Brewood was rather an isolated placed and so was fairly self-contained. Apart from the many farmers who lived in and around the village, Brewood had numerous grocery shops, butchers', boot and shoemakers', and even two watchmakers'! There was a post office and a sub-branch of

Lloyds Bank, which opened every Tuesday afternoon, and the village police sergeant and an assistant constable kept the peace. For such a relatively small settlement there were five public houses, and beer and spirits could also be purchased from three private houses.

Apart from the National School that John Brodie took over as head, there was a separate school for Roman Catholics, the long-established grammar school and at least three private schools all serving the educational needs of the children of Brewood with, it must be said, varying degrees of competency. For a young schoolmaster who had never been considered top-class, Jack Brodie appeared in the first instance to have really fallen on his feet by securing the headship at Brewood National School. It is probable that his fame as an international sportsman may have helped in impressing the school managers and Revd Williams (the vicar of Brewood), and the fact that his new wife was also an experienced elementary school teacher may have meant the Brodies were too good a package to pass over. Eda Brodie was to run the infant school. However, Jack Brodie's experience and skills as a teacher must have been the deciding factor in his appointment, because Brewood National School was a school in trouble.

A scheme for a national school in Brewood started as early as 1816, and by 1818 money had already been raised towards providing a room for the 'daily instruction of 350 children'. By 1834, around 140 children were being educated in Brewood National School and the numbers in 1851 had risen to about sixty boys and fifty girls, 'under a master and mistress'. The school received an annual government grant from 1858 onwards, and two years later the school and master's house were constructed, with a local wealthy family named Monckton bearing half of the cost. In 1870, the school inherited a bequest of £2,000 stock from the estate of a clergyman called Kempson, who at one time had been the headmaster of the grammar school. His will stated that half of the interest from the bequest was to be 'applied to the school'. The provisions of the will also stipulated that the schoolmaster, mistress, and children must attend Divine Service 'as might be appointed on saints' days in Brewood church, and the attendance of the pupils for religious instruction on one Sunday in every month'.

Despite being a wealthy institution and enjoying popular support from the people of Brewood, the school was in a bad way when Jack Brodie took charge on 9 January 1888. There was a total lack of exercise books (then called 'copy-books') for the pupils to work in and, to his horror, Brodie found no English grammar had been taught for seven months. Likewise, the girls at the school had received no instruction in housecraft during the same period. Brodie asked the vicar to oversee tests in arithmetic and writing for all the children in the school to establish the pupils' academic knowledge and capabilities. The results reflected the poor teaching experienced at the school prior to Brodie arriving in the village, with a mere quarter of the 120 children tested reaching acceptable levels in numeracy and only a third writing reasonable English. These results were so poor that Jack Brodie decided that the course of instruction the pupils had been receiving since the previous summer would have to begin afresh, even though the usual end of year exams were less than five months away.

With over 140 girls and boys registered to attend the senior part of the school, Brodie only had two partially trained teachers to help him, and there were major concerns about their competence. In his logbook he wrote that one of his staff (a pupil-teacher named Leonorah Till) had 'been as much neglected as the children, for in an exam in Arithmetic she could not get a single sum right'. With such poor support it is easy to see why Jack Brodie had his work cut out, and why he did not contemplate returning to playing football for the Wolves sooner. However, his headaches at school were compounded further by the poor behaviour of many of the children and the lack of support shown by their parents. Things must have been concerning him when he noted after only a week in the post that 'the habit of running home from school among the children seems to be rife'.

It must be remembered that at the time that Jack Brodie was trying to establish order and turn his school into a calm place of learning, the notion of compulsory education was still a relatively new concept in Britain and there was still resistance to it in some areas. The Forster Act of 1870 may have set up elementary schools, but attendance had not been made a legal requirement until 1876. Many of the families Jack Brodie had to deal with in Brewood were poor, often itinerant, agricultural workers who would ideally want their children to join them in working the land to subsidise the meagre family income in the same way they had with their parents a generation earlier. Many of them could not see the longer-term benefits that education would have upon the lives of their children and resented having it forced upon them.

It did not take long before Jack Brodie's resolve to bring order to the school was put to the test, but he was up to the challenge. After only three weeks in charge, Jack Brodie expelled a boy in the Standard VI class (about twelve years of age) for using 'filthy and indecent language' to younger female pupils. Although he later readmitted the lad, after reassurances about future conduct had been given to the school managers (i.e. governors), the message had been made clear to the children. Jack Brodie was in charge and poor behaviour would not be tolerated! Although he had set out his stall, Brodie had to maintain high standards of pupil behaviour, and was not averse to taking strong action to do so. On one occasion in his first term in charge he noted in his log that he had punished a boy for stealing. He added:

> This boy steals nearly everything he can lay his fingers on and is capable of being carried away. At the beginning of the week he stole one of the children's dinners and today I discovered he had stolen handfuls of slate pencils out of the box, slates (I have made parents give up two this morning), pens and a knife out of the cupboard. The boy and his brother are fearful thieves and appear to be encouraged at home...

There is little doubt the parents of some of his disaffected pupils resented Jack Brodie's firm approach and tried to get him into trouble. On 1 October of his first year as headmaster he punished a girl 'for repeated and wilful disobedience'. The girl's father wrote to the vicar accusing Jack Brodie of 'having caused his three children to have scarlet fever'. He added that he 'will not have any children corrected by anyone for anything they may do'. An angry Jack Brodie dismissed the charges made against him as 'the most outrageous'. It is easy to see why the youngsters of this family were described as 'the most troublesome children' with such poor parenting behind them. Brodie later had another run-in with this father who was summoned and fined by magistrates for not sending his children to school regularly. 'Out of spite' he falsely accused Brodie of thrashing his son during dinnertime for fighting with his brother. Brodie indignantly stated, 'I absolutely did not see the boy and knew nothing of it until afterwards.'

A tragic incident took place during Jack's early years in Brewood, the memory of which stayed with him forever. He was awakened from his bed one night by an anxious father whose son had not returned home from school that afternoon. Jack tried to help the distressed man by going out with a lantern and searching around the village, but it was not until the next morning that Jack himself found the little boy's body floating in the canal. It seemed the child had gone to play along the canal bank after school had finished, and had fallen into the water. After this, Jack Brodie ensured that he regularly gave the children at the school clear warnings about the dangers of playing near the open waters around the village.

Despite his difficult start at Brewood, John Brodie began to overcome the problems that faced him and gradually improved things. He became the village choirmaster, but his duties as headteacher were increased in the summer of 1892 when ill health forced his wife to give up her position as head of the infants' school. Eda Brodie had been ill off and on for some time and this had caused the younger school children to be kept at home for days at a time. An incident that surely affected Eda Brodie's chances of recovery took place on 22 March the following year. She and Jack were returning to Brewood from the railway station at nearby Four Ashes. They were travelling in Jack's pony and trap with a friend called Gair, who was the tenant at Wooley farm. Approaching Brewood along a narrow lane, they collided with a miller's wagon. The Brodies' trap was smashed and their pony bolted free into the centre of Brewood, dragging the shafts with him. Blaming the miller for carelessness, the *Express & Star* reported that Jack Brodie and Mr Gair had only just avoided serious injury, but 'Mrs Brodie was very severely shaken'. A temporary teacher called Miss North had been employed for over two months while Eda had been unfit, but upon her resignation, John Brodie took responsibility for the infants' establishment and it was fully integrated into the school. The new larger school was renamed Brewood Church of England School, and it continued to be very important in educating the children of Brewood while Jack Brodie was in charge.

As time went on, there is little doubt that Jack Brodie had become a well-established figure in the community life of the village. Recalling his childhood in Brewood at the turn of the twentieth century, Alf Rhodes referred to Jack Brodie's status within the village:

A little further along [Dean St] lived a very important person in the village, the schoolmaster, who owned a large comfortable house. He was Mr J. B. Brodie, an ex-Wolves player of international class...

The house that Alf Rhodes referred to was the accommodation that came with the post of school headteacher and was situated within the school grounds. It was owned by the Church, and the Brodies paid a small weekly rent to live there. For a few short years, up until the time of Eda's death in 1902, it was their family home, and each of their three children had been born there. Despite its spacious accommodation, the house was far from luxurious. Running water was not installed until 1905, at a time when improvements were being made to the school building. A year later, John Brodie vacated the house and it was let to a new infants' teacher named Arthur Bill who was charged a weekly rent of 5s. Brodie and his daughter Phyllis took up residence in another house in Dean Street, where they were looked after by a housekeeper named Annie Shenton, who originally hailed from Dover in Kent.

All of the Brodies' children followed their parents' calling of teaching at one time or another. In 1904, the eldest Brodie son (John Lockley Brodie) was articled as a pupil-teacher under his father's tutorage. After three years of 'on-the-job training', the younger John qualified and joined the staff of the school. He only stayed in teaching for a further three years, before responding to an advertising campaign in the local press and emmigrating to Canada to take up a post at the Imperial Bank. A year later he was joined by one of his father's brothers, who also sought better opportunities in the 'New World'. He was a great loss to the village school, and was presented with 'a case of razors, a fountain pen and a pocket knife' by the children when he left the school for the last time. John Lockley Brodie settled in Canada, working for the bank in the township of Welland in Ontario. He married a girl called Mary Josephine Gordon, but, like many others, his life was totally disrupted by the outbreak of the First World War in August 1914. As a nation of Dominion status within the Empire, Canada declared war on Germany and her allies in support of Britain. Young John Brodie answered the call to arms and recrossed the Atlantic, now as a soldier. While stationed in Britain before crossing the Channel to the Western Front he most probably visited his family in the Midlands. After surviving the horrors of the war he returned to Canada, but sadly died in 1920 at the age of thirty-three.

The middle Brodie child was Harold, who was born in the autumn of 1893. He occasionally taught as a pupil-teacher at Brewood, but his heart was never really in it. He eventually moved to Wolverhampton and made a living buying and selling cars. He lived in the Bradmore area of the town, but later moved to Womborne.

The baby girl of the family was Phyllis, who was baptised on the penultimate day of the nineteenth century. She was barely four years old when her mother died of pneumonia. As a young teenager Phyllis taught the infants at her father's school and remained with him well after he had left Brewood. She eventually married and moved to an area south of Birmingham, where she died in 1970.

It is safe to say that once he became established, Brewood School, under Jack Brodie's leadership, was a very busy, vibrant and lively place. The average weekly attendance just before Brodie took over was 140 girls and boys and 60 infants and in 1894 attendance averaged 154. The high numbers being taught continued well into the new century. For example in 1910, 35 infants and 122 older children attended the school on average each week.

The school was quite wealthy in comparison with many other similarly sized schools. In 1905 the school's income from Kempson's endowment was £50, which by order of the Charity Commissioners was that year 'wholly assigned to the general purpose of the school'. This was in addition to national funding, and so in Brodie's time Brewood School was well off. The school itself was a long, single-storey brick building, situated near the south end of the Market Place. In 1907 the accumulated balance of the trust fund was assigned for improvements. These were needed because up until that time all the children had been taught in a single large room, with Jack instructing the boys at one end and a mistress working with the girls at the other. With the numbers involved, it must have been very noisy at times. Separation of the boys and girls classes was needed, especially as the school mistress was charged with teaching needlework to sixty-three girls at any one time. In 1906, school inspectors recommended 'a glass and wood partition should be put in the main room'. In 1906 there was a separate classroom for infants, but it seems that these children had a poor experience of school. The educational needs of the younger children had never really been met since Eda Brodie's time. Due to the persistent absence of the pupil-teacher who had responsibility for the infants, Brodie's female assistant had to absorb the younger children into her class, meaning on occasion she was trying to teach well in excess of a hundred children.

Over the course of time, Jack Brodie seems to have developed into a fine headmaster. The inspectors had reported in the autumn of 1905 that 'the school continues to be conducted with much skill and its general tone is all that can be desired'. The report from the following year indicates how Jack Brodie approached his work: 'By his genial manner and kind but firm discipline, the master [Brodie], has gained the complete confidence of teachers and scholars alike, with the result that much excellent work is done in the school.' The report went on, 'The school is well organised and no effort is spared by the master to keep his work up to date.' This was in sharp contrast to the school he had taken over as a young headteacher back in 1887.

Some of the education children at Brewood National School received under Jack Brodie was surprisingly modern considering the time. In 1904 he went on a part-time course, gaining a First Class Pass in the Horticultural Exam for Teachers and established a school garden in land off Dirty Lane. The following year he agreed to let his school take part in the 'Norfolk Scheme'. This was a programme for the teaching of mathematics to children from agricultural communities. The inspectors deemed that the scheme was 'an interesting experiment', and commended the school for taking part in the project. Considering Jack's background, it is not surprising that the inspectors also noted 'the Physical Exercises were another strong feature of the school's work'. The inspector detailed how Brodie approached this aspect of his teaching: 'All the movements were well done, there was praiseworthy steadiness between the movement and great care was taken to make the children understand the purpose of each movement from a physiological and hygienic point of view.'

Even in his final year at Brewood Parish School, Jack Brodie had lost none of his enthusiasm for his calling. In April 1912 His Majesty's Inspector of Schools wrote of Brewood School, 'The headteacher devoted himself to his school and it is quite a pleasure to talk with the children in all parts of the school, but particularly in the master's own class.'

Jack had become immersed in the rural culture of village life in Brewood. Not only were many of the lessons he taught concerned with agricultural training, but he himself became very interested in beekeeping. He must have been good at this, as he won prizes for the honey he had made in several village shows held in Brewood in the final years before the First World War.

After living and teaching in the village for more than twenty-five years, many local people must have been greatly surprised when Jack Brodie announced his intention to resign the headship at Brewood in the summer of 1913. As he wrote his last entry in the school logbook on 29 August that year, Jack must have experienced some very mixed emotions. Over the previous quarter of a century he had become a well-established, respected figure in the community who, through his hard work and dedication, had changed and improved the lives of very many children. He had raised his family in Brewood and watched as two of them flew the nest. His poor young wife and childhood sweetheart lay dead in the local churchyard, but maybe now Jack Brodie needed change in his life.

In the spring of 1913, he had been approached by members of the Staffordshire County Education Authority who wanted him to become the head of a newly built school in Woodfield Avenue in Penn, just outside Wolverhampton. The new school was state of the art for the time, and the authorities wanted an experienced but enthusiastic head to take charge. It suited Jack to move back nearer to his adopted home town, as he wished to renew his involvement with his beloved Wolves, and indeed had recently been offered a directorship of the club. If the new post and directorship were not enough, Jack also had a major change in his personal life in that year, because in October 1913, at the age of fifty-one, Jack Brodie remarried.

His new bride was a widow named Judith Sarah Wills (*neé* Turner). Judith, the daughter of an Anglican clergyman, had originally come from London but had lived in the Leeds area for many years. She had settled in Brewood in the 1890s with her husband Arthur, a surgeon and general medical practitioner who had originally come from the Merridale area of Wolverhampton. The couple had lost a daughter in childhood, but also had a son named Arthur Gerald Wills who attended Brewood School, and most probably that was where the Jack first met Judith. Sadly, her husband Arthur passed away in 1910 and Judith moved to London. She and Jack kept in touch and they married in the capital in that last year of peace before the First World War started. The people of Brewood were sorry to see their popular headmaster leave. A public appeal was launched and quickly enough money was raised to purchase a 'fine roll top writing desk'. Jack was invited to return to Brewood a few months later, where he was publically presented with the desk by the vicar of St Mary and St Chad's. Upon leaving Brewood, Jack and the new Mrs Brodie moved into a fine Edwardian house on Mount Road. No. 4 was only a quarter of a mile or so from the site of Baynton's Windmill Field, where Jack had first played football almost forty years before.

The Staffordshire Education Committee and the Church of England Diocese of Lichfield were rightly proud of the new school on Woodfield Avenue, although when it officially opened on 1 September 1913, many of the new pupils had to be housed in temporary classrooms, as the main buildings had not been finished. It had been planned that the school would accommodate children from the expanding suburb of Upper Penn, as the nearby schools of St Phillip's in Bradmore and St Bartholomew's near Penn Common were both old and overcrowded. The chairman of the governors was a clergyman named Cox, who had known Jack Brodie for many years, and under his watchful eye Jack eagerly took on the task of organising and managing the school. Woodfield Avenue opened with a roll of 107 boys and girls, but it was intended that eventually over 300 would be taught at the school. Jack Brodie had a staff of three teachers to assist him and individual classrooms were light and airy – a sharp contrast from his first days at Brewood! At Jack's insistence, a garden had been laid out within the school grounds so that his new pupils could learn about horticulture and plant growing.

Initially the school did very well and, at 99.1 per cent, Jack Brodie was quietly proud that his school had the best attendance rate in the district. However, there were some teething problems with the building in the first term. Poor caretaking meant that the heating system did not work properly throughout the winter months and the temperature in the school seldom rose above 47°F, meaning 'the children, particularly girls, were working in discomfort'. They must have got over this temporary blip because as the weeks passed by in that first year at Woodfield Avenue School, life settled down into a regular routine for both the staff and children. The roll increased as children were transferred from the old Bingley Street School, but the new children were assimilated into the developing community of Jack Brodie's school without any major problems. The children seemed to take to their new school well, as Brodie and his colleagues were both good educators and popular. They believed in rewarding good work and effort, and Jack permitted his charges to have 'free games' (as opposed to organised formal PE lessons) when there were instances of 'no scholar being late this week'. Extra-curricular activity was seen as important; the school entered choirs into local competition and on Monday nights Jack regularly took the boys swimming after school had finished for the day.

It was a good time of hope and innocence, and the little school in Penn was a happy place. However, like the golden summer days that ended Woodfield Avenue's first year, things were about to change and it would not be for the better.

War clouds were gathering over Europe and the storm they heralded would impinge on the lives of millions all over the world. The little community in the quiet backwater of the suburb of Penn would not be spared the effects of the coming maelstrom.

A few days after Britain declared war on Germany and her allies, term started at Woodfield Avenue. Jack Brodie addressed his pupils in assembly and told them of the courage and sacrifices that the country would need to make in order to overcome the enemy. The children sang the National Anthem and the Union flag was put on display in the school. It would be there for the duration of the conflict for over four long years.

Although Jack had the clear aim of keeping the children focused on their studies, the excitement of events in France and Belgium were at the forefront of everyone's mind. The thrill of older brothers and cousins heading to the hall of the Congregational chapel on Snowhill or to Broad Street for medicals to answer Lord Kitchener's call to 'join the Colours' must have seemed like the start of an exciting adventure to the little ones still at school. Undoubtedly, versions the early skirmishes of the great conflict would have been re-enacted in the playground a thousand times over. The Germans would be defeated and it would all be over by Christmas. Everyone said so, but as subsequent events showed, the late summer of 1914 was a time when leaders, soldiers and civilians all over Europe were quite naïve to the horrors and hardships that modern war would bring, and the demands it would make on everyone.

Jack Brodie's interests and experience as a teacher put him in a much better position than many of his contemporaries to channel his pupils' patriotic enthusiasm into constructive activity. He encouraged the children to turn the school garden into a vegetable plot, and by the end of April 1915 they had harvested over 400 cabbages, which were sent to the village in Stone (north of Stafford) for distribution 'amongst less-favoured schools'. Whether the children of Stone fully appreciated all that cabbage is not recorded, but at a time when the war was getting on for a year old, all food was precious.

As the First World War progressed into its second full year, new accents and languages could be heard in the classrooms as eight refugee children from Belgium were taken into the school. Five of these youngsters belonged to the Da Haes family and they had suffered terrible hardships fleeing the advancing Germans in their homeland the previous autumn. Their relief at the sanctuary they found in Jack Brodie's school can only be imagined, but in truth the war was never really far away. At the beginning of June 1916 regular lessons were suspended so that the children could receive government-promoted teaching on the 'War Economy' and 'How to Help Win the War'. Pamphlets were distributed to help drive the message home. Only two days later, on 9 June, Mr Gregory (the attendance officer) left to join the Army and within a week he had been joined by Mr Davis, who had been one of Brodie's best teachers. Although both men survived the war and returned to their duties at Woodfield Avenue in 1919, Gregory was tragically killed when his motorcycle collided with a car in November 1922 while he was visiting the home of an absent child at Jack Brodie's request.

Through the difficult summer months of 1916, with the Battle of the Somme raging in faraway France, Jack managed to keep the children working and learning, and despite many problems the school had some notable successes. Two girls and two boys passed entry examinations to the town grammar schools and the standard of education the school provided was praised in inspectors' reports. However, in spite of this good news, many children were losing loved ones in the vicious fighting on the Western Front. Jack had formed a good working relationship with 'Dr Barnardo's Young Carers League', who visited bereaved children and consoled them. However, Jack Brodie had his own tragedy to deal with in the autumn of that year.

On Bonfire Night 1916, Judith Brodie died of exhaustion in Granville House on Tettenhall Road. Granville House was part of the town's women's hospital, where she'd had a hysterectomy the previous week for cancer of the uterus. For the second time in his life Jack Brodie had been widowed. The marriage to Judith had lasted only three years, and had not been the happy saunter into old age that they had hoped for, but Jack was not completely alone. He had a large extended family living in Wolverhampton, and a successful haberdashery shop established by his mother still operated in the town centre. Shortly after Judith's death, Jack moved to a fine Victorian house on the Penn Road called 'The Nook'. His new home was closer to the school and Jack's son Harold moved close to his father and saw him often.

Life at the Woodfield Avenue School continued in much the way it had since the outbreak of hostilities in 1914. Collections of gift boxes and magazines for soldiers were regularly made and Brodie continued to lead by example. He gave the pupil-teachers model lessons to help with their training, and had to act as a supportive father figure when one of his women teachers received a War Office telegram informing her that her brother had been killed in action on the Western Front.

In November 1918 the guns finally fell silent. The occasion was marked at Woodfield Avenue when 'the children marched past and saluted the Union Jack which had been erected in the girls' playground, after which they sang Kipling's Recessional Hymn and the National Anthem'.

As everywhere else in Britain, it was a time of reflection and hope for the future, but the end of hostilities did not mean the school's problems were over. Only a month after the Armistice was signed, the widespread and virulent Spanish Influenza epidemic finally hit the Penn area of Wolverhampton. On the instructions of the Ministry of Health, Jack Brodie closed the school – with over half the 215 pupils suffering from the malaise there was little point in trying to stay open. It was not until over a month later that the situation was considered favourable enough to reopen the school.

Outside school, Jack was still very active in the affairs of Wolverhampton Wanderers. Having been invited back onto the board of directors in 1913, he must have hoped that the team would have been able to ascend into the top of the two divisions that made up the Football League at that time, and live up to the potential the club had shown only five years earlier when, against all the odds, Wolves had lifted the FA Cup for the second time. Despite some notable performances, the flowering of the Wolves team of 1913 into a real contender for promotion was cut short by the outbreak of the First World War in August 1914. Football became very unpopular with the general public, as many club directors – working on the assumption that the war against Germany would be a short-lived affair – were unwilling to release players from their contractual obligations to join the armed forces. Wolves came in for greater criticism than most when it was decided that 'friendly' football matches using 'guest' players should continue to be played at Molineux, even when the FA suspended all official competitions in 1915. The directors of Wolves tried to placate popular disquiet about their decision by allowing Molineux Grounds to be used for the military training of volunteers and the holding of public meetings.

There were high expectations for football in Wolverhampton after the end of the First World War. The men who had returned from the horrors of the trenches were more demanding, far from the subservient boys who went to France in the service of their country. They expected to be thrilled and entertained by the Wolves and would not put up with second best.

The first full playing season after the war saw Wolves slump after a promising start. They seemed to be in danger of relegation to the newly created Third Division, and there was much grumbling and discontent on the terraces, especially after Wolves suffered a massive 10-0 defeat to Hull City. Matters came to a head on 18 October 1919. In only the fifth game to be officially held after professional competitive football had resumed at Molineux, Wolves were pitted against Bury FC. The two teams had met at Bury the previous week and the northerners had won by a single goal. At the Molineux match the visitors were again ahead by a goal when, controversially, they were awarded a penalty. The home crowd was so incensed by the referee's decision that several hundred invaded the pitch and 'the man in black' was forced to flee towards the safety of the changing rooms. Unfortunately, he slipped to the ground and was quickly surrounded by the irate mob. The players attempted to protect him, as the police on duty in the ground that afternoon were easily outnumbered, and disaster was only avoided when Jack Brodie and some of his fellow directors went onto the pitch and appealed for calm. Eventually, police reinforcements were summoned and order was only restored after the chief constable threatened to read the Riot Act. The referee was corralled in the changing room and only spirited away after darkness had fallen.

Jack Brodie's courageous action and his disregard for his personal safety meant he emerged from the affair with great honour and his integrity intact – but not so the club and its supporters. The Football Association showed its displeasure by imposing a fine on the Wanderers and ordering the closing of the Molineux for two home matches, the games to be played at an alternative venue. The actions of the supporters had cost the club £1,000 in gate receipts and advertising revenue and, to their ever-lasting shame, Wolves fans had to watch their team turn out for the fixtures against Barnsley and Stockport at the Hawthorns – the home ground of fierce local rivals West Bromwich Albion!

Reaching the cup final in 1921 was the one bright spot in a time of general decline, and the years that followed were really traumatic for the 'Old Gold' club. The final was the fourth occasion since their inception that Jack Brodie was able to go with his Wanderers, and experience the pinnacle match of the English game. Unfortunately, the game against Tottenham Hotspur, held at Stamford Bridge on St George's Day 1921 in front of 74,000 spectators, resulted in a win for the Londoners.

A lack of new faces in the dressing rooms and an over-reliance on older players gave the strong impression that the board lacked the ambition to bring greatness and success back to the club. This view was unfair, as it was undoubtedly true that Jack and his colleagues on the board craved success as much as the next man, but the local economy was suffering in the aftermath of the war and financial resources were not easily come by. Jack Brodie's contribution to the running of Wolves in those changing and challenging times was probably more to do with nostalgia than hard-headed business dealings. The club that he had started was now a serious commercial concern, and the complexity of its dealings was probably way beyond both the experience and knowledge of the schoolmaster, even though it was said that his quick wit and good humour did much to enliven the often dull and mundane business of routine board meetings. However, this did not placate disgruntled followers of the team, and a supporters' group was formed. Public meetings were held at which a change in the running of the club was demanded.

At the end of the 1922/23 season, matters came to a head. Wolves finished the season in their lowest position ever and were ignominiously demoted to the Third Division (North). Calls for the creation of a 'public liability company' to raise funds and run the club became overwhelming, and the old board (including Jack Brodie) was dismissed. No longer involved in the running of the club, Jack still showed his love and loyalty to the Wolves by purchasing £5 worth of shares in the newly formed company. The changes the new arrangements heralded were long overdue, and had beneficial immediate and longer-term effects. Within a year Wolves (1923) had won promotion back to the Second Division and only three seasons later had appointed one of the most iconic footballer managers of the pre-war era –Franklin Charles Buckley. In his seventeen years in charge, Major Buckley would make Wolves one of the most famous clubs in Europe and discover many great players such as the legendary Stan Cullis and Billy Wright.

There seems little doubt that it was at school that Jack Brodie felt most at home. As the 1920s came roaring in, the country was still recovering from the First World War. It might be thought that the school in Woodfield Avenue, which Brodie had guided through the great conflict and the terrible influenza epidemic that followed might be due a period of calm and stability. But turbulent fate had not finished with it yet.

A severe outbreak of measles hit the school in May 1920, resulting in almost a third of the pupils being away from their desks. The disease was described by Brodie as 'a bad type accompanied by bronchitis and other chest complaints'. It must be remembered that at the time children would not have been in good physical condition to resist infection, due to the lack of nourishment and the privations they had experienced during the previous years of conflict.

The school attempted to engage the children in pleasant activities to take their minds off the harshness of their young lives. In July 1920, Jack granted them a half-day holiday so they might visit and enjoy the Wolverhampton Flower Show, but the year was to end on an unhappy note. To everyone's great shock and consternation, Gwendoline Newman, a promising student teacher being mentored by Jack Brodie, suddenly collapsed and died.

Despite all the problems Jack had faced in both his professional and private lives, he continued to give of his best to the children in his care, even though at about this time his own health began to suffer. It is said that he had walked with a pronounced limp since an injury in the latter stages of his football playing career had damaged his right knee, but now, approaching sixty years of age, he started to experience problems with his heart. However, with suitable medication he continued with his work and even expanded his outside interests. In 1920 he joined the local Freemasons, becoming a member of the Tudor Lodge.

Despite all the problems that might have defeated a lesser man, Woodfield Avenue thrived under Jack Brodie's leadership. In 1922, a school inspector named Hartley wrote that despite the school being very overcrowded (an average class size of fifty-three), the problem was 'discounted by the adoption of methods which concentrate on individuals rather than big groups'. Implementing what was effectively a 'child-centred' approach to teaching, as an educationalist Jack Brodie was again decades ahead of his time. The report went on, 'There is further an admirable system of free classification which allows every scholar to move up the school at his own natural pace, a plan which has been undoubtedly justified by its results.' Jack and his teachers were producing well-rounded and eager learners from children who had been through a great deal of difficulty. Hartley recognised the school's achievements when he wrote, 'Indeed, one of the outstanding features of this successful school is the ready response of the scholars to the calls on their initiative, diligence and sense of responsibility.' The report noted that the school enjoyed the 'goodwill of the parents who take a keen interest in the doings of the school and who assist in many material ways the work of the teachers', and that many children volunteered to do homework. But perhaps the greatest praise was reserved for the headmaster, Jack Brodie:

> Much of the undoubted success of the school is due to the headmaster's personality and influence, which are felt in every department. He continues to show the greatest personal interest in educational developments so far as they affect both the general welfare of the school and his own teaching, inspiring his staff by precept and example, with the same enthusiasm.

This was the final report ever written on Jack Brodie and marks the zenith of his professional career. He had developed into an excellent educational leader and manager, who was admired and respected by his pupils, their parents and colleagues alike. Just as in his days as a footballer, he truly made a beneficial difference to the people he came into contact with, irrespective of their age or social standing. Hartley's comments were an accurate reflection of the character and personality of Jack Brodie and the value of what he brought to the lives of others in terms of organisation, inspiration and example.

By the end of 1924, Jack was having an increasing amount of time away from school with poor health. So much so that by the end of January 1925, he was forced to hand over temporary charge of the school to Mr Davies, one of the more experienced assistant teachers at Woodfield Avenue, while he took a leave of absence due to illness. Just two weeks later, on the 16 February, Mr Davies made the following entry in the school logbook.

Mr Harold Brodie visited the school this morning bearing the tragic news that his father, Mr J. B. Brodie, our respected headteacher had passed away … After communication with the managers and the Central Authority at Stafford it was decided to close the school this afternoon.

Jack had passed away peacefully that morning, aged sixty-three, and news of his death quickly spread beyond Penn. The following appeared in the minutes of a meeting of the board of directors of Wolverhampton Wanderers that took place the next evening: 'A note of condolence was passed to the relatives of Mr J. Brodie. It was also decided to forward a wreath and the players on Saturday to wear black bands.'

On a cold February morning, only three days after his death, Jack Brodie was laid to rest alongside his second wife, Judith, in the town cemetery at Merridale. Children and staff from Woodfield Avenue attended the funeral service and his cherished school choir sang hymns as his burial took place. They had joined surviving members of his family, including three of his brothers and his son Harold, as well as members of his lodge. Wolverhampton Wanderers' directors and representatives from the Football Association were also in attendance at the service, as were old friends and men he had played football with so many years before. They had come to pay their last respects not only to one of the founders of the club, but 'one of the finest gentlemen Wolverhampton had ever produced'. His old mate Jack Baynton was among them.

There is now little to remind the curious of Jack Brodie's passing. His gravestone has been missing for some years and his final resting place can only be found by carefully searching the registration numbers on the remaining stonework. But his legacy is far, far more than a few words inscribed on a stone in a graveyard. Brodie was never a rich man in terms of money (indeed, his surviving son Harold inherited a little over £3,114 from his father after probate had been settled), but Jack left the people of his town a legacy worth much more than gold or silver. He left them the Wolves.

From the backstreets of Blakenhall he, Jack Baynton and their friends, by enthusiasm and hard work, had started the process of establishing the team by which the name of the town was borne throughout the world – Wolverhampton Wanderers.

Every generation has popular cultural heroes, be they sporting, military, entertainment, political or other, and it is hard to appreciate their importance and significance once they have passed on. So perhaps the final words on Jack Brodie should be from someone who knew him. This was a sports journalist called John Catton who worked for a publication called *All Sports*. In the early 1920s, Catton wrote of the Wolves:

What famous footballers this club has produced. Their names convey nothing to the modern enthusiast, but 'Jack' Brodie, schoolmaster, centre-forward, captain, 5 ft 9 ins, 12 st 3 lb, with a pink cheek, a mass of black curly hair, and a voice that exhorted cheerily, 'Come on lads!' was a sight and a sound that boded woe to the antagonists.

Times were different then, but in Brodie's day it was not uncommon to see the full-backs felled, the goalkeeper on his back, and the ball forced between the posts in one pell-mell rush.

There were great men on the ball and famous teams before many of us were born. All honour to the pioneer clubs, which have kept their banner flying.

Woodfield Avenue
Woodfield Avenue School opened in 1913, and Jack Brodie's last headship was based here. (Author's collection)

Wolves' First Trophy
Wolves with their first trophy, the Wrekin Cup, 1884. (WWFC collection)

Above: Wolves at Dudley Road
The Wolves first XI at the Dudley Road ground,
c. 1889. The black armbands worn are a mark
of respect for Jack Brodie's late father, Hugh.
(WWFC collection)

Left: Wolves' Coat of Arms
Wolverhampton's original coat of arms and
Wolves' first club badge. (Author's collection)

William Barcroft
William Barcroft and pupil-teachers at St Luke's, *c.* 1875, with Jack Baynton (*back centre*) and Jack Brodie (*back, extreme right*). (Gask family collection)

The Nook
The Nook, Penn Road. (Author's collection)

The King's Arms
Wolves' first headquarters and changing rooms. (Author's collection)

Headmaster's House
The headmaster's detached house in Brewood. (Author's collection)

Above: The Blacksmith's Shop
The blacksmith's shop, now demolished, at
the front of the Mermaid Inn, Wightwick,
c. 1875. This was the birthplace of Jack
Brodie. (Author's collection)

Right: Jack Brodie
A sketch of Jack Brodie as the Wolves'
captain, *c.* 1889. (Author's collection)

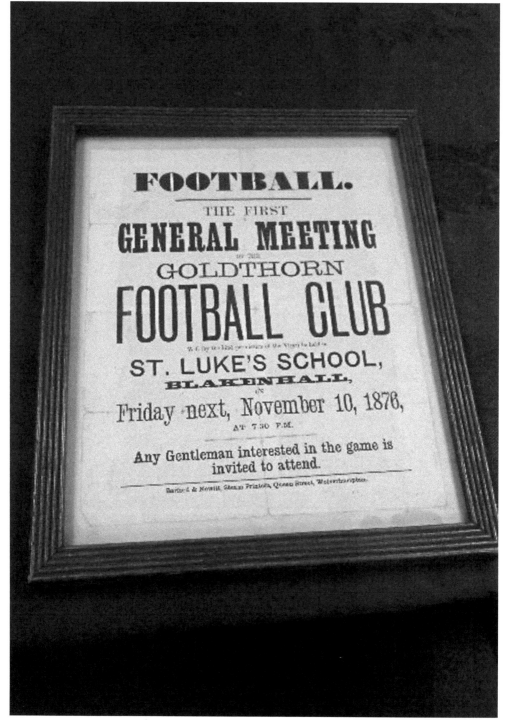

Original Calling Notice

The calling notice, dated 1876, inviting 'interested gentlemen' to join the Goldthorn Football Club (Wolves' forerunner club). (WWFC collection)

Above: Molineux Grounds, *c.* 1895
Molineux Grounds from the hotel
end looking north-west, *c.* 1885, with
evidence of rubble from the demolition
of the original formal gardens.
(WWFC collection)

Right: Jack Brodie, Captain
A portrait of the captain of the Wolves
in full playing kit, *c.* 1889.
(Author's collection)

Left: Jack Brodie, Headmaster
The headmaster of Brewood National School in
1912, standing outside the main school doors,
aged around fifty. (WWFC collection)

Below: Headmaster Brodie and Pupils
Jack Brodie (*left*) posed with a group of pupils at
Woodfield Avenue School, *c.* 1924.

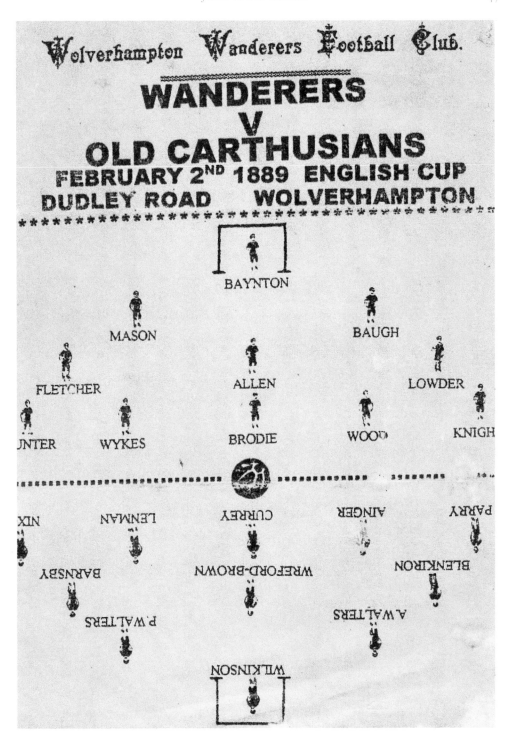

Early Wolves Match Card

An early match card detailing the team line-ups from the 1888/89 season match against Old Carthusians. (WWFC collection)

Above: Brewood in the 1890s
A street scene from the village of Brewood.
(Author's collection)

Left: Levi Johnson
A posed head and shoulder portrait of
the Wolves' treasurer. (Wolverhampton
City Archives)

Arthur Hollingsworth
A head-and-shoulders studio portrait of
Arthur Hollingsworth. (Wolverhampton
City Archives)

Alfred Hickman
A studio portrait of Wolves' first president.
(Wolverhampton City Archives)

No. 3 Haggar Street
The Brodies' home in Haggar Street, Blakenhall. (Author's collection)

2

JACK BAYNTON
'The Delightful Baynton'

As he made his way from the graveside on that cold winter's day and headed up Jeffcock Road towards his home in Penn Fields, Jack Baynton must have reflected deeply on the passing of his old friend, John Brodie. As at every funeral, the mourners would have swapped stories and talked about the deceased, and Jack Baynton had a good few tales to relate about Brodie – a man he had first got to know over half a century before. Even in those far-off days when the old queen, Victoria, was on the throne, they had really 'hit it off' and had formed a friendship the years would not break. After all, the two had a lot in common.

They had both been christened 'John', although everyone had called them 'Jack'; neither of them had been born in Wolverhampton, but came to regard the town as 'home'. Both of the boys came from large families and they both chose to follow careers in education, (initially at least). However, the bond that held them tightest was their enduring love of sport, especially the game of football.

Born on 20 March 1859, Jack Baynton was older than Brodie. Baynton first saw the light of day in the small Worcestershire village of Rushock, which is situated about 3 miles from Kidderminster. At the time of his birth, Jack's father, Samuel William Baynton, was farming a 96-acre spread with the strange name of 'Hagmans and Worms Field'. Samuel originally came from the north Staffordshire village of Stone, and must have been a successful businessman, as it is recorded that he 'employed labourers' on his rented farm. Jack's mother was called Martha, and was eleven years younger than her husband. Jack was the fifth child (second son) of the nine she was known to have borne Samuel before his death in 1872.

When Jack was barely a year old, his father took over the tenancy of Lodge Farm, which lay to the south of Goldthorn Hill on the edge of Wolverhampton. Spread over 200 acres of rolling countryside, Lodge Farm was much larger than Samuel's holding at Rushock had been. It is likely that Martha Baynton and John Miller (who had lodged with the Baynton family at Rushock and oddly enough was a miller by trade), who both came from Sedgley, would have been aware of its availability through family who still lived in the vicinity.

Lodge Farm was what was known as a 'mixed' farm, and with the aid of four labourers and an apprentice, Samuel Baynton raised not only cattle and a few pigs, but also grew cereal crops such as corn and wheat. There was an old windmill at the extreme southern edge of the farm in the 1870s, and the land adjoining this mill became St Luke's first football pitch. Samuel died on 19 November 1872, and although Martha and her older children attempted to maintain the tenancy of the farm and keep working the land, they do not seem to have been very successful and only managed to keep the business going for a further few years. It appears that although Samuel had not left a formal will, Martha was his sole executor and received all her late husband's assets and effects, estimated to be worth 'less than £1,000' by the Probate Office. Although this may seem a lot, much of it was tied up in farm machinery, feed and livestock. It must also be remembered that the farm was a business of significant size, and most likely Samuel would have had financial liabilities stemming from normal trading activity. To expect Martha, a forty-year-old mother of nine, to be able to pick up where her husband had left off and do equally well would have been impossible. Within a few years of Samuel's death, Martha and her family moved to Haggar Street (just a couple of doors from where the Brodies were living) and Lodge Farm was taken over by a relative named Charles Baynton. (It seems that Charles did not stay long at Lodge Farm. By 1881 the land was being worked by a shepherd named Thomas Ward, who came from Northfield in Shropshire.)

Martha worked hard to keep the family housed and fed, but with so many children it was understood that they would have to find work as soon as they were old enough. One of Jack's older sisters, Sarah, was taken on as a pupil-teacher at St Luke's School in the infants' department in January 1873, but ill health forced her to leave the school after just a few months. At the age of just thirteen, Jack was to follow her into the school as a monitor and 'candidate' for the post of pupil-teacher on 9 January the following year.

The primary school that Jack joined had officially opened in March 1862 with an attendance of eighty-seven, although it had operated elsewhere during the previous year. The first headmaster was named Forbes, but in January 1873, a young Saltley College graduate named William Henry Barcroft took charge of the school. Despite his inexperience, 'Harry' Barcroft was expected to bring education to local Anglican children with just the help of a few teenage pupil-teachers, such as Jack Baynton and later his friends Jack Brodie and Jack Addenbrooke.

Pupil-teachers usually started their five-year apprenticeship after a short period of being a 'monitor'. Monitors were expected to watch over pupils only slightly younger than themselves and instruct small groups. In Anglican schools, if they impressed the headteacher and the supervising vicar, they would be offered a position as a pupil-teacher.

The concept of 'pupil-teacher' emerged in Britain in the mid-nineteenth century, when there were moves afoot to establish basic primary educational provision for young children. Pupil-teachers were one of four officially designated types of instructor that could be found in schools, the others being 'principal teachers' (headteachers), 'assistant teachers' (i.e. qualified staff) and 'probationers' (who could serve a maximum of two years after their pupil-teacher apprenticeship had ended). To gain acceptance as a pupil-teacher, it was decreed by the Privy Council that a candidate must be at least thirteen years of age and have no 'constitutional infirmities', such as curvature of the spine or an arm or leg missing. Rather helpfully, the Privy Council pointed out that 'a hereditary tendency towards insanity' would be 'regarded as a positive disqualification'! Schools would receive financial support from the government for employing up to four pupil-teachers at any one time, and St Luke's attempted to benefit from the system by appointing only one or two each year, so that there would always be trainee teachers working in the school. In the first year of training, a pupil-teacher was paid £10 (subject to an inspector's approval), but by their final year they received twice this amount. By comparison, the headmaster (who had to be a college-trained teacher) was paid for training pupil-teachers and could supplement his annual salary of £25 by up to an additional £15. The pupil-teacher trainer at the school was expected to give at least an hour's instruction to the trainees every day, in order to prepare them for an annual test supervised by a visiting inspector. Only pupil-teachers who gained a First Class Pass in their final inspection were allowed to enter teacher training college and thus avail themselves of the better career prospects possession of a teaching certificate could bring.

Pupil-teachers were expected to instruct between forty and fifty 'scholars', but it must be remembered that, at the age of thirteen or fourteen, they were only a little older than their charges. Maintaining discipline and giving sound instruction must have been well-nigh impossible to young lads like Baynton and Brodie. Working in an educational system whose greatest merit was that it was relatively cheap to operate, it is understandable that pupil-teachers were often less than enthusiastic about their work and many gave up before qualifying. The government laid down what the apprenticeship teacher should be able to do effectively at each stage of training. Competency ranged from being able to read fluently and have knowledge of basic weights and measures in the first year, through to being able to 'compose an essay on some subject connected to the Art of Teaching' in their final year at the school. As well as acquiring skills and knowledge to utilise in the classroom, pupil-teachers had to gain an annual 'Certificate of Good Conduct' from the school managers, and a statement from the head that their attendance, punctuality, 'obedience and attention to duty' had all been satisfactory. Only if they received this approval, and a letter from the vicar that they had been 'attentive to their religious duties', were pupil-teachers allowed to continue onto their next year of training.

The St Luke's School that Jack Baynton joined as a monitor, and later as pupil-teacher, was not an easy place to work in. Even before Barcroft took over, his predecessor complained in 1866 that 'many of the boys are very lazy' and later, 'the boys in the First Class are very idle today and very troublesome. I caned several of them.' Seven years later, when Barcroft was installed as headmaster, behavioural problems were still evident. On 17 January 1873, just eleven days after Barcroft's appointment, St Luke's vicar, Revd Parry, paid the school a visit and reported that 'maps should be used in geography lessons and discipline needs a little more attention'. On the same day, Barcroft wrote in the school logbook, 'I had to punish several boys for insubordination.' He later added, 'Kept about thirty boys back during the break for a breach of school discipline.'

Harry Barcroft was not only faced with difficult pupils as he attempted to establish St Luke's School as a seat of learning; the professionalism of some of the staff left much to be desired. He noted in the logbook in 1874, 'E. J. Hampton (a pupil-teacher) absent from lessons on Thursday without any other reason than "that he preferred to stay at home"'. Despite such poor role models, Jack Baynton's apprenticeship got off to a good start. Within weeks Harry Barcroft recorded 'Baynton satisfactory in timekeeping and work', but it was not to last. On 8 May he noted, 'Baynton absent from lessons.' It was the start of a pattern of absenteeism and poor punctuality that was to be repeated throughout Jack Baynton's time as an apprentice teacher at the school. Nonetheless, on 15 January 1875 he was formally accepted a pupil-teacher. Barcroft wrote, 'John Baynton and Charles Walton commenced their apprenticeships.'

Whether Jack Baynton had become complacent now that he was a paid member of staff, and felt that the school needed him more than the other way round, is not clear. It may be that as a young teenager he lacked emotional and guiding support, coming from a family that had no father and an overburdened mother, to fully concentrate on undertaking his work and duties at the school. What is clear, however, was that his actions worsened when his friend and neighbour Jack Brodie joined him at the school. During the ensuing months, even years, the school logbook records Harry Barcroft's despair with his young trainees; comments such as 'Baynton late for lessons every day', 'John Baynton without lessons on Monday morning, J. Brodie the same' and 'Baynton absent from lessons again on February 27 without leave' were typical entries made by the young headmaster. Barcroft tried to improve the situation by recommending that the school managers employed a more experienced teacher to mentor the boys. A former pupil-teacher from nearby St John's School named Alfred F. Pinfield was taken at 10s a quarter (paid quarterly), whom Jack Brodie was to assist as a monitor. Barcroft believed this addition to his staff would have a beneficial effect on his younger members of the school workforce. He wrote, 'He [Pinfield] seems a thorough worker and will, there is no doubt, give satisfaction.' However, Jack Baynton was not to improve by subtle suggestion or observation. Barcroft needed to apply stronger measures. On the 17 April 1875 he noted, 'On Tuesday found J. Baynton's class very backward. Placed J. Hewitt into the classroom and removed J. Baynton into the large room under the direction of Mr Pinfield.'

Despite such serious steps, neither Baynton's nor Brodie's performance improved greatly over the course of that summer. They were often late for school or did not turn up at all. On several occasions Barcroft noted, 'John Baynton and John Brodie's work not finished and what was done was unsatisfactory.' It may have been that their minds were elsewhere. Perhaps they were preoccupied with their new passion – football!

Despite their many shortcomings, both lads could produce acceptable work when they put their minds to it, but it seems they found it hard to maintain the effort. Barcroft noted that an improvement in the work of his teachers took place at the beginning of 1876, and in spite of the occasional return to bad ways, the two Jacks worked hard until the June of that year when they were examined by the visiting Government Inspector of Schools. Both boys were considered to have made sufficient progress to carry on to their next year of teacher training. It would appear that Alfred Pinfield's guidance and advice had benefited the young pupil-teachers, and his influence had been felt throughout the school in general. Sadly, he left the school at Easter 1876, and Harry Barcroft was to sorely miss the support he had provided. This was not the only problem facing St Luke's School at the time. The provision of state education might have been a fairly novel idea, but it was not free. Families were expected to pay a penny each week for every child who attended elementary school. For the better off, 'school pence' bills could be paid quarterly. In March 1876, Jeremiah Mason, the local councillor and philanthropist who had provided land for both the church and school sites, was in dispute about his bill and refused to pay. Barcroft wrote that he 'decided to enforce payments' through legal means. The matter was eventually resolved, but caused some unpleasantness within the tight-knit Anglican community of Blakenhall.

Without Pinfield's mentoring, both Jack Baynton and his younger friend Brodie reverted to their previous habits of poor timekeeping and sporadic absenteeism. Barcroft attempted a new approach to remedying the situation. He tried to ensure that both his errant trainees would feel pressurised by their charges to turn up to lessons on time: 'Pupil-teachers to their classes an hour late. Boys kept in until five o'clock to make up for lost time on Thursday.' Barcroft's strategy of punishing the pupils for their teachers' misdemeanours failed miserably, as the following day he wrote, 'On Friday morning J. Baynton was half an hour late for lessons.'

During the autumn term of 1876 and the spring term of the following year, Harry Barcoft's patience was worn very thin by the actions of the two boys from Haggar Street. In fairness, both Baynton and Brodie probably thought the next annual scrutiny by Her Majesty's Inspector was a long way off, and with the arrogance of youth believed they could make up any lost ground nearer to the date of the examination. It might seem odd that the headmaster did not take firm action against either or both of the youths. It may have been that dismissing them from their posts was not economically viable, as they were both partway through their training and appointing replacements to start from scratch might have been seen as wasteful. Also, it is not certain whether there were many young men of a similar age or disposition living in the area wishing (or indeed able) to commence a career in education. The majority of Baynton and Brodie's contemporaries were employed in the local iron industry and, with the plethora of small foundries and workshops nearby, seemed to be assured of better-paid employment for the foreseeable future. Alternatively, it could well have been that Harry Barcroft was a kindly man, who realised he was dealing with teenage boys and did not want to take actions that might have ruined their future prospects. Whatever the reasons, more draconian measures were not taken against the trainees, but matters did reach a point where Jack Baynton was given what effectively amounted to a final warning. On 18 August 1877 Barcroft wrote, 'Both teachers and boys rather slacking with work and the discipline has suffered by the holidays. John Baynton is not punctual to lessons and neither has he then well prepared. Unless he takes more pains, he will have to give up teaching.'

Both at work and beyond the school gates, the two Jacks were all but inseparable and were often to be seen roaming the lanes and byways of Blakenhall and Goldthorn Hill. As with many young men at the time (and since) sport played a very important part in their lives, especially as there were few alternative pastimes for lads of their age in Victorian Wolverhampton. It was certainly true that there were a number of theatres and music halls in the town centre, but they were some distance away and the expense of travelling to and attending a performance would have made a trip 'up-town' more an occasional treat than a regular occurrence. There were plenty of public houses to be found in the area where the boys were living, but it is very unlikely that they would have ever gone into licensed premises, even though the law was far more lax about the age when drinking was permitted than it is today. Anyway, at the time the growing importance of the idea of social 'respectability' meant that pupil-teachers seen drinking in public would have created a scandal, and certainly would have lead to disciplinary measures being taken by the school. (Even some thirty years later a pupil-teacher being seen smoking at a Wolverhampton railway station was extensively reported in the leading local newspaper.) Sport was a way to run off the exuberance, enthusiasm and energy that these young men had in abundance. The long-established and widely played game of cricket was their first love, but they became more and more drawn to the emerging and exciting sport of 'football'. Teams were being successfully established in different parts of the town, but especially at large industrial concerns such as the Great Western engine works on the Stafford Road. Then, as now, it seems to have been the case that where groups of young men gathered together – be it in a workplace, college or church – sporting teams would form and compete with others. For both Baynton and Brodie, pretty much of the whole of their social life revolved around their friends, family and of course, St Luke's parish, and it was natural that this was where they would form their football team in 1877. The church boasted a choir, which met not only at divine service on a Sunday, but also during the week for practice. Many of the members of the choir were former pupils of the school, and it was this group of friends that was to form the first St Luke's team.

Jack Baynton played a full and active part in the team that first formed in 1877. Being slightly older than many of the other club members, he was considered to be one of the more experienced and organised, which placed a great deal of responsibility on his shoulders. Not only was he appointed the first treasurer of the new team, but he had the honour of being the club's first captain on the field of play. At 5 feet 9 inches (although in photographs from the time he appears taller), very fit and healthy, Jack Baynton was a good man to have in the team, and his hard work, enthusiasm and keenness did much to inspire the others who joined the St Luke's team. It is not known if the legend that Harry Barcroft gave Brodie and Baynton their first football with which to organise games in the school yard has any truth in it. However, what is certain is that the head appreciated Baynton's athleticism, as shortly after the football team was formed he got the young trainee to teach gymnastics to all the boys at the school.

With his mind distracted by the running and organising of the St Luke's team, Jack Baynton's general work in the classroom continued to be erratic in quality during the spring of 1878. On 23 April, the head wrote in the logbook one of the few positive entries he made about Jack Baynton's work: 'Examined John Baynton's class with a satisfactory result,' but he added, 'I have had to complain of the teachers' lessons generally all week.'

The school at the time was an unhealthy place to work, as many of the pupils were prone to illnesses rooted in their poverty and insanitary living conditions. Barcroft referred to this when he noted that 'owed to the prevalence of fever, I have had the school disinfected'. To add to his troubles, he was still finding Jack Baynton a difficult trainee to manage. Developing the habit of punctuality to work still seems to have been Baynton's main shortcoming. After he had been late for school four times during one particular week in the autumn of 1878, Harry Barcroft felt he had 'again been obliged to warn John Baynton with regard to extreme unpunctuality'. The head seems to have been quite a hard taskmaster and demanded good results from his apprentices. On 9 November 1878 he 'found the First Class rather backward in Composition and Spelling. Teacher J. Baynton.' However, he added that the pass rate from the test he gave Baynton's class was a credible 86 per cent. It seems he was a hard man to please.

In spite of all the concerns headmaster Barcroft had about Jack Baynton (and to a lesser extent his friend Jack Brodie), both passed the visiting Government Inspector's examination for the year, and were allowed to enter the next year of their training. By now Jack Baynton was well past the halfway point of his apprenticeship and, despite continuing to give cause for concern, he seems to have adopted a more mature approach to his duties from that time onwards. In the first week of February 1879 Barcroft complained that Baynton was 'very irregular at lessons', but on 14 February reported rather sceptically that 'John Baynton says that he intends to work at private lessons more steadily and he is the only teacher whose work has been unsatisfactory'. Actions will always speak louder than words, and it seems Barcroft had little faith that Jack would change his ways. Imagine his joy, then, when just one week later he was able to write, 'John Baynton has succeeded in being present at lessons every morning this week and has only been late once.' The renewed effort paid off for Jack Baynton, as in the third week of April 1879 both his and Jack Brodie's work was inspected and deemed good enough to allow them to continue as pupil-teachers (fourth and third year respectively).

In May in 1879 Barcroft felt confident enough to give the young man a little more responsibility as he reorganised his staff: 'Placed John Baynton in the classroom and have been obliged to have John Brodie's class near my own owing to his continued talking with other teachers.'

There were a few falls from grace as spring rolled on into summer 1879, but John Baynton seemed to have realised that he was approaching the final phase of his training. The teacher training system in operation at the time meant that if he was able to obtain a First Class Pass in his final examination by the Government Inspector – and get financial backing from the Diocese – he would be eligible to apply for teacher training college in the way that Harry Barcroft had done before him, and his friend Brodie was to manage a year or so later. Only with a recognised qualification from a teacher training college of the period would Jack Baynton eventually be able to become headmaster of his own school. It seems that Jack was willing to make a final effort to complete his training period with as high a pass as possible. On 13 September the logbook recorded 'John Baynton had leave of absence – two half days – to prepare for the Examination Certificate.' Just a week later Barcroft acknowledged the effort the young man was making, but expressed concern about Jack's chances in light of his long-term overall performance:

Sept 18th John Baynton is working very hard for his Examination, but he cannot think a fortnight's work can in any measure offset a year's neglect. His work in school is everything to be desired but his attainments show 'lack of interest' in home study.

It was not really surprising that this was the case. By the time Barcroft recorded those thoughts, Jack Baynton was without the supportive family network he would need for studying at home, and it was most likely that to all intents and purposes he was fending for himself. In the late 1870s, his widowed mother Martha had taken up the position of housekeeper for a thirty-eight-year-old widower named John Reade and his fifteen-year-old daughter. Reade was the tenant of a public house in the Staffordshire hamlet of Bilbrook, which is located some 4 miles north-west of the centre of Wolverhampton. When she moved from Blakenhall to the Greyhound Inn at the top of Lane Green Road in Bilbrook, Martha took her youngest three children with her. While living at the pub, Jack's younger brother, Frederick, managed to get work locally as a shop assistant, while the youngest Baynton girls, fifteen-year-old Louisa and thirteen-year-old Flora, worked as a dressmaker and a 'confectionary apprentice' respectively. Louisa and Flora were to stay with their mother long after all their siblings had married and set up their own homes. Eventually the three of them moved to Denbighshire in Wales to run a boarding house.

It was around the same time as Jack was approaching his final months at St Luke's that he started courting, and this was sure to have proved a distraction to the young man. His friend Jack Brodie and his family had moved to No. 21 Shaw Road in nearby Coseley. Just three doors away from their new home, at No. 24, lived a family called Smith. Like most Victorian families living in and around Wolverhampton, the Smiths were a large household. Again, like most of his local contemporaries, the head of the family, Daniel Smith, worked in the iron industry until his death in 1878. Having lost his wife some years earlier, the main duties in looking after the home and family fell to his eldest daughter, a young woman called Harriet. Harriet Smith had been born in Heath Town and was three years older than Jack, but the stability and care she was to bring into his life was something the young teacher seems to have really needed when the pair married a few years later.

Back at St Luke's, Jack Baynton's praiseworthy efforts continued through the autumn term of 1879. On 18 October his Class Three were examined by Harry Barcroft who reported, 'Everything satisfactory but grammar.' But alarm bells started to ring as he entered his penultimate term as a pupil-teacher. In the second week of January 1880 Barcroft noted that although Jack had been absent through illness, his class had been 'very disorderly throughout'. With his final assessment only few months away, the head expressed concerns over Jack's reversion to his bad old ways: 'J. B. has not shown the energy. He will fail either in the work or order [of his pupils].'

Despite Barcroft's misgivings, Jack Baynton seems to have made a renewed effort during the final months of his apprenticeship. In the final 'teacher's monthly report' of 1880, which referred to Baynton, Barcroft wrote in quite glowing terms, 'John Baynton – great improvement with regards to punctuality. The last month seems to be entirely fixed upon his work. The order of his department has been praiseworthy and in consequence the work of the boys is the same.'

The following month Baynton was examined by the inspector; although receiving a credible pass, his work was not deemed good enough to be recommended for entry to teacher training college. It seems too many absences and instances of poor punctuality during the previous five years had had their effect on his overall achievement, although it is unlikely that Baynton would have had the financial support from his family that a successful student boarding away at a college would need anyway. Instead, he would have to seek an alternative way to further his career. The only route open to him was to become a 'probationer' at another Anglican elementary school. With few family ties and little to keep him in Wolverhampton, Jack Baynton headed for Birmingham, where he obtained employment as a master at All Saints School in the suburb of Hockley.

On 26 March 1880, Barcroft wrote in the school logbook, 'John Baynton has left the school, as his apprenticeship terminated on the 25th.' However, this would not be the last he would see of young Baynton by a long shot.

When Jack Baynton departed from Wolverhampton, not only did he leave his good friends around Blakenhall, but also the Goldthorn football team he had been instrumental in forming only three years before. His contribution and influence on the young team may have been missed, but enthusiastic others were coming to the fore to ensure the club survived and flourished. Brodie would still be about for another year, until he left for Saltley Training College, as were other founder members of the club such as Fred Blackham and John Henry Addenbrooke, both of whom were also pupil-teachers at St Luke's. Under the watchful eye of the club president, Alfred Hickman, and with the support of well-wishers such as Jeremiah Mason and Levi Johnson, the infant club flourished.

Jeremiah Mason had better reason than most to support the fledgling club. His third-born son, Charles, was one of the first St Luke's lads to put his name forward to join the Goldthorn team in 1877. Charles (or 'Charlie' as he universally known) had been born in April 1863 to Jeremiah and his wife Anne, and was educated at the school that his father had been so involve in establishing. When Charlie left St Luke's, it seemed that he was destined to join one of his older brothers, John or Edward, in the japanning or tin trades; but at the age of fourteen he was far more interested in the new sport of football. Charlie Mason developed into a left-back of rare quality. In a football career spanning fifteen seasons, he was to turn out for the team over 300 times, a third of which were FA Cup and later League appearances. Not only did Mason have the distinction of playing in both the first cup and League fixtures of the club he had helped form, but he has the unique honour of being the first Wolverhampton Wanderer to be selected to play for his country. In all, he played for England on three occasions. While at Wolves, he formed a formidable defensive partnership with Dick Baugh. Like Brodie and Baynton, he retired from football in his mid-twenties only to return to the game later. In September 1887, the local paper celebrated his return to the team: 'The followers of the favourite winter game [i.e. football] will learn with pleasure that "Charlie" Mason has yielded to the unanimous wish of many friends, and will again join Baugh at "back" for Wolverhampton Wanderers.'

When he finally retired from the game in 1892, Charlie Mason became a 'puddler' in a local foundry. He continued to live in Wolverhampton until his death in 1941.

Like his friends Mason and Brodie, there is little doubt that as a young man Jack Baynton enjoyed participating in team sports. He was a fine cricketer and was to play the game well after he hung up his football boots in the 1890s. As a teenager he was tall and athletically built, and the fact that he was to play in eight different positions for the St Luke's team (and the Wolves team that emerged from it) bears witness to his enthusiasm for the game. With many of the earliest Wolves matches being small-scale, localised and unreported affairs, little is known of Jack's prowess on the field of play when the team first started. A tale about Baynton's football performance from the time has survived the years and gained the status of legend among historians of Wolverhampton Wanderers. Many report that Jack Baynton scored a goal direct from 97 yards out! (The exact distance is known because apparently the match was stopped so that astonished officials could take measurements.) It is likely that Baynton scored this famous goal straight from a goal kick. He acted as goalkeeper for the team on a number of occasions and made the position his own in the latter stages of his Wolves career.

While he was teaching in Birmingham, Jack Baynton returned to Wolverhampton to visit friends and family on many occasions. On the day the official census was taken in 1881, Jack was recorded as a 'visitor' with his mother at the Greyhound public house in Bilbrook. Oddly enough he also appeared as a 'visitor' at Harriet Smith's home on the same day. With little but work keeping him in Birmingham, and with a developing romantic relationship back in Wolverhampton, he decided to return to the town. Within a year he had left All Saints School and his digs in Hockley and gone back to Wolverhampton, but not to Blakenhall. Instead, he moved in with Harriet's family, who had left Shaw Road and moved to New Zoar Street in the neighbouring district of Graisley.

In the summer of 1882, having gained a 'Third Class (Division Two) Teaching Certificate' from successfully completing his probation in Hockley, Jack sought work as a fully qualified teacher in Wolverhampton. Despite there being other Anglican schools close to where he was living, he returned to St Luke's. Perhaps it was a little surprising that Harry Barcroft should want to employ his former erstwhile trainee, but Jack Baynton was a changed character. During his time in Birmingham, he had not only gained a lot of valuable experience in his chosen profession, but he had matured both socially and emotionally. By this time Jack had become engaged to Harriet, and the stability and security he gained from the relationship was something that had been missing from his life during the years he had been a pupil-teacher. From Jack's point of view, returning to St Luke's had a number of benefits. He was fully aware of how he school was organised and what Harry Barcroft and the school managers would expected of him, but above all else, it meant a return to his old friends and the great love of his life – the Wolves.

On the 8 May 1883, Jack married Harriet at St Paul's church on the Penn Road, with her brother and sister acting as witnesses. Jack and his new wife moved into a small terraced house in nearby Mander Street. It was the start of a happy and long marriage that was to last well over half a century. The year 1883 was memorable for Jack Baynton for other reasons. With its two founding members, Brodie and Baynton, returning to the town like Biblical prophets of old coming back to the 'promised land', the Wolves pack was back together and about to start on the road to becoming one of the most famous teams in the history of the game. It was in the 1883 football season that Wolves entered the FA Cup competition for the first time, and the one in which they won their first-ever trophy – the Wrekin Cup. The team consisted of William Caddick or Issac Griffiths ('Little Ike') in goal, Tommy Cliff and Charlie Mason as full-backs and a forward line of James Hill, Arthur Lowder, Ted Hadley, John Griffiths (Ike's brother) and, of course, Jack Brodie. Jack Baynton played at centre-half alongside Thomas Blackham, whose brother Fred had been one of the original members of the Goldthorn team. His sister, Lucy, had been a pupil-teacher at St Luke's at the same time as Brodie and Baynton.

On the 27 October, Wolves played their first FA Cup tie against Long Eaton Rangers and, in front of a crowd of over 2,000, came from behind to win four goals to one. After such a good start, Wolves travelled to Wednesbury for the next round, but were beaten 4-2 by 'Old Athletic' – probably the best team in the Black Country at the time. Far better progress was made in the Midlands-based Wrekin Cup, with Wolves beating St Paul's (Birmingham) by 7-0. In this match Jack Baynton showed his versatility as a footballer by playing in goal for the Wanderers.

By the end of the season, with a first trophy to their name, Wolves was a flourishing club with twenty players on the books and more local lads eager to join. However, as the club went into the next season Baynton's place in the Wolves line-up seems to have been assured. Although they only played in one round of the cup before being knocked out by Derby St Luke's after a replay, Jack played in both matches. In the first of the encounters, he played on the forward line as Wolves' inside-left, but reverted to centre-half for the replay at Derby on 22 November 1884.

Although Jack and his teammates had completed thirty-five fixtures that season, the November match would be the last FA Cup game that Baynton would play for the Wolves for three seasons, although the reasons for this sabbatical from football are not clear. It is true that he was taking on a lot more responsibilities in both his personal and professional lives, and this may explain why he had less time to devote to football. In 1884, Jack and Harriet became parents when their daughter Violet Ethel was born. Violet Baynton was to be Jack and Harriet's only child. She was educated at St Paul's elementary school in Merridale Street in Wolverhampton. She later became quite a successful actress and starred as the 'Fairy Queen' in the production of *Dick Whittington* staged at the Shakespeare Theatre in Liverpool in 1909. She subsequently married a Londoner from Brixton named Herbert Linley Jones, whose father, Sidney Jones, was a famous writer of musical theatre productions such as *The Geisha*. The couple had two children, but Herbert was to die in the service of his country in the final months of the First World War in 1918. Violet remarried the following year to a Wolverhampton man named Arthur Whitehouse. They stayed in the Penn Fields area of the town for number of years before going to live in Alfreton in Derbyshire.

At St Luke's, Jack gained experience and skills as a fully qualified classroom teacher and manager, and Harry Barcroft came to rely on his support more and more. Although there was no designated post of deputy headmaster at the school, it was in effect what Jack Baynton became over time. The school logbook refers to several instances where Barcroft was away and left the 'school in the charge of John Baynton CM [Certified Master]'.

Another reason why Jack may have left the club for a while is that he was suffering because of the Wolves' growing success. Like Brodie, he was only ever an amateur player, and as such could claim nothing but expenses – even after his return to the side in 1888/89 season, when Wolves played their first full League season and reached the final of the FA Cup, Jack Baynton only received £6 7s 6d in expenses for twenty-four games played. As their prowess grew, Wolves became involved in matches and competitions much further way from Wolverhampton than had been the case when they first started. Although he might not have been out of pocket playing for Wolves, the commitment would have certainly taken up an increasing amount of his time. For example, a trip to play at Stoke or Preston, even by steam train, would have taken up virtually the whole of a Saturday.

As competitions took on more significance, the Wolves' growing army of supporters would have become increasingly critical of instances of underperformance. This became a time when an individual's enjoyment of a game was surpassed by the significance of the result. It is not known how any of the players in those far-off days dealt with fans' expectations and reactions, but for any man to give up his free time, unpaid, and yet be on the receiving end of critical comments was a lot to expect.

The final, and possibly the most important, reason that Jack took a break from football was a purely practical, financial one. The game of football is a physical one and has always involved 'player contact'. This was more so the case in the 1880s when opponents could be 'shoulder charged and bundled off the ball'. Injuries were common and Jack Baynton had his fair share, but the terms of his teaching contract were such that pay would be withheld if he had time away from school through injuries caused by playing football. With no insurance to fall back on in such an eventuality, and with a wife and child to feed and shelter, Jack could not take the risk of becoming injured while playing for Wolves. Jack might have considered giving up teaching and becoming a full-time, paid football player, as the whole issue of professionalism in the game was a hot topic of public debate at the time. However, a couple of important factors might have dissuaded Jack from even considering such a dramatic career change. Charles Crump, the former Stafford Road team captain and very influential with Wolves players, fiercely opposed the introduction of payment for players and, as in the case of cricket, saw a purity of spirit in the sportsmanship of the unsullied amateur game. Also, it must be remembered that Jack Baynton was well into his mid-twenties at that time and it was uncertain how long a career in football might last, or indeed whether he would make enough money from playing to last him beyond the short term.

In the final season before the advent of the Football League in 1888, Wolves had had a fairly dismal run in the cup, and although they had beaten two local sides in earlier rounds (Walsall and Aston Shakespeare), they were unceremoniously dumped out of the competition on 26 November 1887 by fierce rivals West Bromwich Albion, who won 3-0. Despite this, they had done well in other competitions and had only been defeated nine times in forty competitive matches. The Wanderers' goalkeeper for the season had been a player called Llowarch who had previously been with Wolverhampton Rangers. Llowarch had replaced the popular 'Ike' Griffiths, who had retired from the game the previous summer, but he himself was not available to stay with Wolves after the 1887/88 season had ended. With many more games coming up in the forthcoming season, the vital position of 'the man between the sticks' had to be filled quickly. On behalf of the committee, club secretary Jack Addenbrooke approached Jack Baynton to attempt to coax him out of retirement to rejoin the pack. With the assurance that adequate private insurance against injury would be provided, ever-loyal Baynton answered his club's call in its hour of need and agreed to become the first XI goalie. Rejoining Wolves in 1888 may not have been a hard decision for Jack to make. By that time he had been teaching at St Luke's for six years and, despite being trusted and given extra responsibilities by Harry Barcroft, he knew that his lack of college training and qualification meant that the much better-paid role of headmaster was beyond his reach. It was more than likely that Jack Baynton was becoming tired of always playing second fiddle and, increasingly disillusioned with teaching, he was keen to use his talents elsewhere.

In a kit of a red-and-white-striped shirt and blue shorts, and totally indiscernible from other members of the side, Jack turned out for the first home League match against Aston Villa on 8 September 1888 at Wolves' Dudley Road ground. According to reports in the local paper, Wolves had the better of the first half, with goalkeeper Baynton only being called upon to deal with a 'feeble try' from Villa's Green, which he 'easily averted'. After Villa had 'wakened up', Wolves were put under a lot more pressure and had to thank Baynton for still being in the game: 'Garvey (Villa) dribbled the ball right through the Wanderers back up to the goal, and Baynton by a brilliant display of goalkeeping cleared his position.' Wolves went ahead through a deflected own goal scored by Villa's full-back Gershom Cox, but the visitors evened the score when Tommy Green 'glided the ball' in off the goalpost, past Jack Baynton, just before the half-time break. Despite continuing into the second period, neither side scored again, but the crowd of almost 3,000 left the ground knowing that they had seen a bravely fought contest in which Jack Baynton had been well worthy of his place. Jack was back – and he was enjoying it!

Jack Baynton kept his place in the team for the next seventeen Football League games, during which time he managed to keep a clean sheet on three occasions. However, in the remaining fourteen games he had the ball put past him no fewer than thirty-two times. The heaviest of these defeats came on 27 October 1888 when Preston North End, the super team of the age, played Wolves at home. In front of a partisan crowd of 10,000, the 'Invincibles' of Preston, as they were widely know, put five past Baynton, with Wolves only scoring two in reply.

On the positive side, Baynton was in goal when Wolves played a friendly game against Manchester East End in November. Wolves won by a staggering nineteen goals to one, but after a 3-0 away League defeat to Derby in January 1888, Baynton was dropped from League games in favour of a London-born amateur goalkeeper called William Crispin Rose. Billy Rose, who was eventually to become a founder of the Players' Union, had seen service with Walsall Swifts before moving to Preston, from whom Wolves signed him. Rose played in the Wolves' remaining League fixtures, although Baynton kept his place in goal for the season's very successful FA Cup run.

The first round saw Wolves pitted against the previous year's winners, Old Carthusians. After a long, hard-fought contest, Wolves took the honours by running out eventual 4-3 winners. In front of a then record home crowd of over 6,000, the second round saw an easier tie against Walsall Swifts, whom Wolves beat 6-0. A third-round home tie was played on 2 March against Sheffield Wednesday. Goals from Albert Fletcher and David Wykes saw Wolves take the tie, but interest had grown so much in their 'cup run' that over 10,000 Wulfrunians had made their way along the Dudley Road to watch the encounter.

A semi-final match against Blackburn Rovers was held at neutral Crewe Alexander's ground a fortnight later and, after a 1-1 draw, was replayed at the same venue on 23 March. Wolves were victorious in the replay, winning by three goals to one. For the first time in their short twelve-year history, the team had reached the final of the FA Cup.

This was truly a magnificent achievement and when the Wanderers returned to the town they were met at the High Level railway station by thousands of townsfolk who 'lustily cheered the team through the town'. For the first time in its long and eventful history, the town of Wolverhampton had a sporting team to be proud of, and civic pride was to the fore. For a week, a rather reserved 'cup fever' gripped the town and the chances of the team lifting the famous trophy was the talk of the pubs, schoolyards and workplaces. The only obstacle in their way was their opponents in the final – the mighty Preston North End.

The Preston team was truly the greatest in the land at the time. It was a mixture of Scottish, Welsh and English international players, who were easily running away with the first Football League title that season (they eventually took forty points from the forty-four possible that inaugural season). In contrast, Wolves were still very much a local team, four of their number (Lowder, Mason, Brodie and Baynton) tracing their association with the club back to its founding in 1877.

The final was held at 4 p.m. on 30 March at the Oval cricket ground in London, in front of a crowd of 22,250 spectators (a record at the time). The referee was Major Francis Marindin, the president of the FA, with Lord Kinnaird and J. C. Clegg acting as 'umpires'. Until 1891, when they were replaced by linesmen (now assistant referees), Umpires each controlled half of the field of play, but had to have their decisions ratified by the game's referee, who sat immobile on the touchline. Only if the referee agreed with one of the umpires could a goal be awarded.

The Wolves had a robust, physical and direct style of play, which contrasted sharply with the more methodical and organised passing game of the North Enders. Wolves nearly took an early lead when Tom Knight's shot on goal hit the crossbar, but gradually the 'scientific approach' of the Preston team started to make itself felt on the game. At the Wolves' end of the ground, Preston's forward Ross also hit the bar, but the rebounding ball was tucked into the net by their winger Dewhurst. Although Wolves appealed for an offside decision, it was overruled. They were to score a second time before half-time, when Ross shot rather weakly towards the Wolves' goal and Jack Baynton 'froze in mortification as the ball slowly passed between his legs'. In the second half, Preston scored again through Sammy Thompson (later a Wolves player), but by then all hope of a Wanderers revival had passed. Indeed, the score against Wolves could have been much worse, had it not been for two magnificent saves pulled off by Jack Baynton.

When the final ended, so too did Jack Baynton's playing career with the team he helped to found. It was rather sad that his final game had been one he would rather have forgotten, but this should not blemish the years of loyal and devoted service he had given the club. He transferred to the minor team of Kidderminster Olympic, where he played in goal for a couple of seasons before quitting playing for good. It was said that while he was with Kidderminster there was a match in which the team were beating the opposition very easily; he was so bored in goal that he went and fetched an armchair and sat and watched the game while he smoked his pipe! In 1891, he joined the list of referees and for two years officiated in Football League and other matches.

After the thrills and excitement of appearing in the cup final, Jack returned to his rather mundane job as an elementary teacher at St Luke's, but he was growing increasingly unhappy with his lot there. His responsibilities and workload increased when, in February 1891, despite extensive advertising, the managers of St Luke's School were unable to find a candidate to appoint as pupil-teacher. Jack continued to shoulder his responsibilities and on 17 July that year was left in charge of the school, but his interest in his job was waning. Finally, on 13 November 1891, Harry Barcroft wrote in red in the school log, 'Mr Baynton's notice expired.' Just four days later, on the 17 November, Jack Baynton finished teaching at St Luke's and left the profession for good. The following month he was replaced by a former pupil of the school named 'Arthur Hodges, Certificate Teacher', but by then Jack Baynton had started his new career as a 'commercial clerk' with the Wolverhampton manufacturing firm of Bayliss, Jones & Bayliss in the All Saints area of the town near to the Royal Hospital.

The firm of Bayliss, Jones & Bayliss had first been established in Wolverhampton in 1826 by Bilston-born William Bayliss (1803–78). Like many Black Country companies dealing in iron and steel goods, it had expanded throughout the nineteenth century and its growth can be gauged by the fact that in 1876 it was one of the largest exhibitors at the Royal Agricultural Show at Birmingham. At that time, the firm produced a wide variety of goods, ranging from cast-iron vases to hurdles and ornamental metal fencing and gates. However, much of the work of Bayliss, Jones & Bayliss was concerned with making parts for railways, and with the rapid expansion of the 'permanent way' throughout the British Empire, the company went from strength to strength in the last quarter of the nineteenth century. In 1896 the business expanded its manufacturing capacity by purchasing Monmore Iron Works, which included rolling mills and puddling furnaces. The firm was also at the cutting edge of the new technology in electrical engineering, which started to develop in the 1890s, and with so much manufacturing activity taking place it needed to expand its organisational and supportive services, such as its finance and wages department. It is not certain whether Jack Baynton applied for a post with Bayliss, Jones & Bayliss by responding to a recruiting advertisement for staff in the local press, or whether he heard about a vacancy through a personal contact. Switching from a relatively safe teaching post to one that was at the mercy of the fluctuations in the economy was not easy, and undoubtedly required some soul searching on his part. Either way, he took the brave step and joined the firm's 1,500-strong labour force when he started working at their Cable Street site.

The education that Jack Baynton had received had lasted longer and had been of better quality than most of his peers had experienced, and was of great benefit to him when he joined the firm. His mathematical ability, together with the neatness and clarity of his handwriting, were ideal skills for a fledging ledger clerk to possess. Jack and his family certainly prospered from the change in his career. Within a few years they had moved from No. 15 Mander Street to a large, comfortable Victorian terraced house at No. 185 Lea Road. As he and Harriet approached middle age, Jack was able to employ a young domestic servant from London named Annie Evans to help with domestic chores around the house.

Even though he had hung up his football boots in the early 1890s, Jack maintained a very keen interest in sport. He was an avid cricket player for several years before the turn of the century, playing in local leagues and cup competitions for teams like 'Wolverhampton Pickwick', for whom he opened the batting.

As it was for so many of its founding fathers, Wolverhampton Wanderers Football Club was always close to Jack Baynton's heart, and even into his later years he seldom missed a game at Molineux. Tony Gask (Baynton's great-grandson) recalls that Jack would watch Wolves matches from just on the halfway line, almost like a referee from the old days when he had played himself. During his years of supporting his beloved Wolves, he would have seen the great highs and lows experienced by the club during its turbulent first half-century. Apart from the cup final of 1889 in which he played, Wolves appeared in a further five finals during his lifetime. They lifted the famous old trophy in dramatic fashion, both in 1893 at Fallowfield in Manchester (when then current holders and finalists Everton initially refused to hand the trophy over after being controversially beaten by the Wolves), and again in 1908 (when Second Division Wolves, inspired by a young trainee clergyman named Kenneth Hunt, beat the much fancied reigning League champions, Newcastle United, by three goals to one). Countering these successes, Jack would have been well aware of the crises that had taken place over the years that saw the Wolves almost go out of business on more than one occasion. Several severe financial crises had taken place around the turn of the century, and the Wanderers had only survived after benefactors such as Sir Alfred Hickman had bailed them out. The club also came in for a great deal of public and press criticism when the directors refused to close Molineux down for the duration of the First World War. It was argued at the time that even limited and restricted football competitions would do much to bolster the morale of workers in Wolverhampton's munitions and armament factories. Also, prior to the introduction of national conscription in 1916, football matches were seen as ideal vehicles for Army recruitment drives.

But such matters had little to do with Jack Baynton directly, as he was not as deeply involved with club issues in the way that Jack Brodie was in later years. Instead, he led a much quieter and more private life. As he progressed in his career with Bayliss, Jones & Bayliss he was able to move his family to a very fine semi-detached house in Eagle Street at the top of Penn Fields close to a terminus of the town's tram system. The Bayntons named their new home *Min-y-don,* which is a Welsh expression meaning 'the crest of the wave', and it was one of an adjoining pair of houses collectively known as 'Church Villas'. Jack and Harriet spent many happy years in the house and were often visited by members of their small family, including their grandchildren Violet and Herbert (known as 'Bertie') Jones and their younger stepbrother. In time, their families too became regular visitors to the Baynton house. Tony Gask recalls visiting his great-grandparents at their Penn Fields home: 'John was a very tall, handsome, kind man, who would occasionally produce the odd flat toffee for me from his pocket.' Even though he was only about three years old at the time, Tony also has clear memories of his grandmother too. He describes 'little granny' as:

> a tiny, bespectacled wrinkly old lady, slightly severe in a well-meaning kind of way. I was her favourite, and she was the only person to call me Anthony. She would sometimes lead me into a corner, giving me a small present, whispering that I should tell no one.

There was little doubt that, as they moved into their old age, Jack and Harriet remained a close, happy and devoted couple, always ready to help and care for one another. Even though he was very young at the time, Tony recalls, 'Little Granny kneeling at Grandpa Baynton's feet doing up the laces of his big black boots in the kitchen of *Min-y-Don*.'

Eventually, after many years of living and working in Wolverhampton, Jack and Harriet retired and moved to live with their daughter and her family in Alfreton, Derbyshire. The couple lived out their last days in that quiet little town, but in 1939, as war threatened to break out in Europe, Jack became ill.

On 17 May Jack Baynton passed away at the age of seventy-nine. His funeral was reported in the *Wolverhampton Express & Star* on Saturday 27 May 1939. Apart from Jack's immediate family and close friends, mourners included a works manager from Bayliss, Jones & Bayliss called Sutton. His presence at that sad occasion, along with wreaths that had been sent by the firm's directors, was a clear indication of the high regard in which Jack had been held by the company.

Jack's important and significant contribution to the founding of the Wolves was marked by the Molineux club – 'Floral tributes were sent by Wolves directors' – but back in Wolverhampton there was little public reaction to his passing. Most Wolves supporters at the time would have been born well after Jack had turned out for the Wanderers, and there would have undoubtedly been a general feeling that he had belonged to another era, when the sport was not as developed nor as widely reported. Only ten days before Jack had died, Wolves, managed by Franklin Buckley, had appeared at Wembley in the cup final against Portsmouth. Although they had lost the match, Wolves had achieved their highest-ever League position when they finished in second place. The fans had experience a tremendous and exciting year, and eagerly looked forward to the forthcoming season, when surely silverware would be lifted by the men in old gold and black! However, a former Army corporal in Germany had plans to ruin that dream, and Major Buckley's team would never reach such great heights again.

In his last days, Jack Baynton would have been aware of how far his club had come. Like Brodie before him, he must have often been amazed by how the Wanderers had grown and developed over the years, from the little bunch of friends who had first kicked a ball on the Windmill Field. He must have gained a quiet satisfaction knowing that without his enthusiasm, commitment and leadership possibly none of it would have happened, and Wolverhampton Wanderers would not have become the famous team that it was and is now.

Dr Percy Young, the Wolves' first historian, described Jack as 'the delightful Baynton'. His strength, good nature and loyalty to his teammates and the club make Jack Baynton the person that all true Wolves supporters should delight in.

Violet Baynton
Violet Baynton as an actress, *c.* 1910. (Gask family collection)

Min-y-don, Penn Fields
Baynton's house in Penn Fields, Wolverhampton. (Author's collection)

Lodge Farm
Lodge Farm, Goldthorn, prior to its demolition in the late 1960s. (Author's collection)

Jack Baynton, *c.* 1883.
A posed studio photograph of Jack Baynton, probably taken for his wedding. (Gask family collection)

Jack Baynton in Later Life
In his garden at *Min-y-don*, Penn Fields, aged
around sixty-five. (Gask family collection)

Harriet Baynton, *c.* 1883
A posed studio portrait of Harriet Baynton,
c. 1883, probably taken for their wedding.
(Gask family collection)

Baynton and Brodie
The two Jacks, Baynton and Brodie, in cricket whites, *c.* 1876. Baynton is seated and Brodie stands to his left. (Gask family collection)

3

JOHN HENRY ADDENBROOKE
'The Hand at the Helm'

Every well-ordered ship, no matter how big or small, needs a skilled and dedicated helmsman at the wheel if it is not to falter and flounder. So it was for the young Wolverhampton Wanderers club as its voyage to fame and glory got underway, and it was very fortunate to be supported and guided by an organisational stalwart in the person of John Henry Addenbrooke. Whereas many young men might have been quickly and easily bored by the detail and minutiae of administration, Jack Addenbrooke's quiet and methodical approach to the day-to-day running of the club was to be invaluable for almost four decades.

John Addenbrooke was the third and youngest of the Jacks and the only one to have been born in Wolverhampton. His birth was at No. 84 Dudley Road on 6 June 1865, and he was the fourth child of Jane and John Addenbrooke, after whom he was named. The family had moved from the nearby village of Gornal just a few months prior to John's birth. John Addenbrooke senior was described in the census as simply a 'bricklayer', but most likely had higher social status than the occupational title suggests. It is probable that he ran a small construction firm, employing others in building new houses in the area around Blakenhall in the mid-nineteenth century. A family photograph of the time shows John appearing both confident and prosperous – the very essence of a Victorian artisan. Like many couples of the period, Jane and John Addenbrooke had a large family – twelve children in all, who attended St Luke's School. John junior was a pupil at the school when the inaugural meeting of the Goldthorn Football Club took place in 1876. He always claimed to have been the first club secretary, organising matches in the school playground at the tender age of just ten!

After he had completed his schooling, young Jack had not finished with St Luke's. He followed Baynton and Brodie into the ranks of the school's apprentice teachers. On 28 January 1878, Jack's sister Adele's name appeared in school records for the first time, and on 23 August that year Harry Barcroft wrote the following in the school logbook: 'Employed two Monitors at the rate of 2s 6d a week – John Addenbrooke and Fred Blackham.' Both were employed on a temporary basis. Fred's sister Lucy was a pupil-teacher in the infants' department at St Luke's, and he was to become one of Wolves' first players! Jack got off to a good start at St Luke's. In October 1878 the headmaster was pleased to report 'Class 6 Work as usual. Addenbrooke temporary monitor. Shows considerable ability in the management of Standard Three.' Despite such praise, Jack Addenbrooke was unable to progress in his career in education that year, because of the shortcomings of his counterpart, Fred Blackham. At the end of the year a visiting inspector concluded, 'Addenbrooke and Blackham cannot be admitted to as satisfactory monitors as Blackham failed to pass his Standard.' (It soon became evident that Fred Blackham was not cut out for teaching and he left the school soon after to be replaced by a youth called Frederick Walters.) Young Addenbrooke does not seem to have been disheartened by the inspector's decision and continued to try hard. On 21 April 1879 Harry Barcroft wrote in the log, 'John H. Addenbrooke. The teacher has worked hard and successfully during the week. His discipline might be better. His lessons have been satisfactorily done and has been punctual in lesson time.' Things seem to have been boding well for Jack in his efforts to become a teacher, although Harry Barcroft did have some minor criticisms that, in hindsight, seemed to herald future problems. A staff appraisal report dated May 1879 noted:

> John Addenbrooke. The fault of this teacher is that he does not get away from the boys enough during the reading lessons. However, he has good teaching ability and will no doubt do himself credit. I have to complain to his father of his attendance at lesson time on Monday morning.

As Jack Addenbrooke commenced the second and the subsequent years of his five-year training programme, his initial enthusiasm for the role of pupil-teacher seems to have waned. Positive reports such as 'Addenbrooke's work carefully done' became interspersed with comments about his work being unsatisfactory. As he entered the adolescence period of his teenage years, Jack Addenbrooke stated to ape some of the less salubrious aspects of the older pupil-teachers at St Luke's. Punctuality issues became a real concern for poor Harry Barcroft. Despairingly he wrote in the logbook, 'I cannot induce the PTs [pupil-teachers] to come in time for lessons – and am afraid I shall have to alter the times.' To even have to consider changing the times of the school day to accommodate poor timekeeping was bad enough, but more problems were evident when Addenbrooke and the others got into class: 'I have had to complain rather severely about the discipline of the PT classes. They seem to have no idea of order.' Despite his shortcomings, Jack Addenbrooke had both the intelligence and ability to perform well when he needed to. In early July 1883 he spent a week at Saltley College in Birmingham, during which time he sat the entrance examination for the teacher training course. He distinguished himself by obtaining a 'First Class Queen's Scholarship'. He would attend Saltley as a full-time student from the following October. In his final few months at St Luke's, Jack missed a great deal of time at school. Safe in the knowledge that his college place was secure, he seems to have come and gone as he pleased, leaving Harry Barcroft to plead with him to attend regularly. Perhaps one can sense that Jack's heart was not really in pursuing a long-term teaching career, but seeking an alternative was still some way off. Having bid his fond farewells to St Luke's, John Henry Addenbrooke followed in the footsteps of John Brodie and entered St Peter's Teacher Training College at Saltley, with the full support of the Lichfield Diocesan Board of Education.

Jack must have had a real shock to his system when he experienced college life for the first time. The students' day was based on the Victorian virtues of 'early to bed, early to rise', and there was something of a monastic feel to his life at St Peter's. Almost all of the working day had been structured so that there was little opportunity for idleness or the tomfoolery young men often get involved in. Housed in a communal dormitory, Jack and his fellow trainees were woken from their beds at 6.30 a.m., and were expected to undertake private study for an hour. Half an hour's communal praying took place in the college chapel before the students finally had breakfast. From 8.30 a.m through to 1 p.m., the students attended lectures ranging in subject from Euclid and algebra, to Latin and political economy. Not surprisingly, lectures on religious knowledge were central to what was taught at Saltley. The middle of each day was taken up with what was known as 'industrial drill'. This was the general term given to a range of practical physical activities, which could include working in the college vegetable garden or helping to replenish the fresh water supply tank on the roof from a well. At 2 p.m. a filling, but usually unimaginative, lunch was taken in the dining hall. A typical dinner would have been boiled mutton followed by currant pudding, all washed down with watered-down ale (known as 'small beer'). Lunchtime gave Jack a short time to himself, before lectures resumed at a quarter past three. These lasted two hours and an hour's private study occupied his time until tea was served at 7 p.m. This final meal of the day was merely bread and butter, followed by a cup of tea, and any time remaining before bed at 9 p.m. was again taken up with private study.

The conditions that Jack endured at St Peter were best described as spartan. For example, there was little heating in the dormitories and it became common practice for students to place wooden drawers on the counterpane of their bed in an attempt to prevent draughts. It was a far cry from Jack's comfortable family home, back on the Dudley Road in Wolverhampton.

Jack's development and progress in the practice and organisational aspects of teaching was assessed from his endeavours at the 'practising school'. This was a school with a roll of over 100 pupils, which was run and financed by the college. Student teachers not only practised their teaching skills at the school, but also observed model lessons given by their lecturers. Despite some minor shortcomings, Jack made steady progress while at Saltley and took an active part in all aspects of college life. He was a member of the football team and other clubs and societies, and took a keen interest in art. In October 1884, he passed the religious knowledge examination with a Class II grade. In the ensuing months at Saltley he was successful in three modules for drawing, but only one for science. In the final 'governors' examinations' that Addenbrooke sat at Saltley, he came thirty-fourth out of fifty in his year group.

In 1883 Jack joined Wolves as a player, along with two of his brothers. He played as a forward in their reserve side, but never made a first-team appearance. His organisational skills and ability had not gone unnoticed, and it was while he was on summer vacation from Saltley College in August 1885 that he was asked to take on the role of the club's secretary-manager. From the time of its inception, less than a decade before, a committee of eleven elected club members had overseen the running of the club. The committee were a mix of players and supporters, and at the time Jack took up his post it included John Brodie's father, Hugh; James and Fergal Hill; William Caddick; and former old boys of St Luke's, Arthur Blackham and William Lowder. St Luke's headmaster, Harry Barcroft, also sat on the committee, always ready to give his support and advice to the young team. John Baynton was the club captain as well as treasurer, while secretarial duties before Addenbrooke's arrival were undertaken by Thomas Cliff, who was ably assisted by John Lockley (the man who was to become Jack Brodie's father-in-law), both on a part-time and unpaid basis.

Under the presidency of Alfred Hickman, the Wanderers could also cite the patronage of the town's mayor, three Members of Parliament, a lord and a viscount as testament to their growing status. In light of the Wolves' Wrekin Cup and other local competition successes, a more professional and dedicated managerial approach was called for. Football in Britain was changing and moving away from its amateur origins. There was much controversy at the time about the introduction of full-time professional players, and it was only in 1885 that the FA begrudgingly permitted them for the first time in its history. With the sport having evolved into more of a business, it was felt at Wolves that there was an increasing need to have someone with dedicated time and the ability to organise players' attendance at training sessions and matches, as well as liaise with both referees and the Football Association. Despite the role having the flexibility to allow him to still be able to pursue other interests, Jack received a stipend from the club, and so had the distinction of becoming Wolves' first-ever paid official, albeit on a part-time basis.

Upon leaving Saltley College and returning to his parents' home at No. 73 Dudley Road in Wolverhampton in 1886, Jack Addenbrooke managed to obtain a temporary teaching post at Bushbury School. The school was just over 4½ miles from where Jack was living, and he probably got to work either by horse-drawn bus or bicycling. Despite no records existing of his time at Bushbury School, it is known that a year later his contract was made permanent. But this was to be his last as an educator. He left the school in July 1887.

With his income from the Wolves to fall back on, Jack felt confident enough to start a business. On leaving Bushbury School he opened a small tobacconist shop at the southern end of Wolverhampton's busy Dudley Street. As most of the adult male population of Britain smoked at that time, Jack did such a good trade from customers who lived and worked in the town centre that he was soon able to employ an assistant named Kate Hawley to manage the shop while he went about Wolves business. Becoming a very astute businessman, Jack was not averse to using his Wolves connection to advance his trade. He was soon advertising a 'Wanderers' Special' cigar that could only be purchased from his store at threepence each or five for a shilling. He even went as far as to describe his shop as the 'Wanderers' Cigar Depot', and also had card labels produced that could be inserted into the band of a supporter's hat. The cards bore the motto 'Play Up Wolves', while the reverse detailed the name and address of his shop. The little shop had a part to play in the effective running of the club. In the days before telephones were in general use, Jack Addenbrooke contacted players and opponents by letter or pre-printed postcard. With up to five postal deliveries a day, it was a very efficient system, and Jack often wrote to Wolves players instructing them to collect kit from the shop. Typical of such correspondence was a postcard dated 9 August 1891 that Addenbrooke sent to the Wolves' reserve goalkeeper George Moore. He wrote, 'Please bring all your clothes (kit) on Friday to the shop to see what you require for next year.'

For the next few years his business prospered and grew, matching the flourishing of the Wanderers in the latter half of the 1880s. After the cup final of 1889 and the honour the club had received by having an England international game played at its home ground, Wolverhampton Wanderers as an organisation stepped up a gear by becoming 'incorporated' under the Companies Act in 1891. Two thousand £1 shares were successfully offered to the public, and in becoming a 'Limited Company' Wanderers lost much of their original amateur nature. The committee was replaced by a board of directors elected by the new shareholders, although a 'selection committee' remained in place to deal with player and team issues. The influx of new funds did not mean Wolves were without financial worries. Despite increasing gates and further FA Cup success, the club was about to enter a period of economic uncertainty that was to last for many years. It is not surprising really when one considers the usual running costs of a football club, the impact of player professionalism and the widespread practice at Molineux of season tickets being transferred over the fence from supporters in the ground to those still outside to be reused. Finances were not improved by the fact that Wolves only got £10 for winning the cup in 1893, despite the FA receiving £2,559 in gate receipts from the final alone!

Although events at Molineux in the early 1890s were undoubtedly interesting, if not dramatic at times, for secretary-manager Addenbrooke, personal life was also undergoing fundamental change. A short distance from his Dudley Street shop was a public house called The King's Head – one of many drinking establishments that could be found on Wolverhampton's main thoroughfare at the time. The pub was owned by a William H. Anderson, who had a number of such premises in Wolverhampton, but the manager and licensee of the King's Head in 1890 was John Hibell. Hibell was a former resident of Bordsley in Birmingham, and at one time had managed a wire mill in the city. He had a young daughter named Beatrice, who had been born while the family had been living in Wylde Green in Sutton Coldfield around 1869. Beatrice must have caught Jack's eye, and after a period of courtship the couple married on the last day of March 1891 during Easter week. The marriage was to be long and successful, with Beatrice Addenbrooke giving birth to four children over the course of the next twelve years.

Jack Addenbrooke's business in the centre of Wolverhampton had become well established, and by the start of the 1890s he was able to move his business to far more prestigious premises closer to the town's centre – Queen Square. The Square had been known as 'High Green' until 1866 when it was renamed in honour of a visit by Queen Victoria to the town. As Wolverhampton prospered and developed, Queen Square became the central hub of the public transport system, as well as the financial and commercial centre of the town with many major banks establishing branches there. Jack rented a former watchmaker's shop at No. 7 High Street (later incorporated into Dudley Street) just a few yards off the Square for his business, and he and Beatrice started living in a small suite of rooms above the shop. It was here that the young couple started their family, with Beatrice giving birth to two daughters during the course of the next five years.

A short time later, away from his new shop, there was a move to make Jack's role even more central in the affairs of Wolverhampton Wanderers. Since Wolves had moved to the Molineux Grounds in 1890, the hotel had had an important part to play in all club activities. It had provided the team with changing rooms and acted as club headquarters, but even after the local brewery of Butlers had bought the premises from Northampton Brewery in the early 1890s, Wolves were only tenants of the grounds, despite Molineux Hotel being vital to their operation. In 1896, Jack was presented with an opportunity to widen his commercial interests without affecting his new tobacco shop in the town centre. In the August of the previous year the town's magistrates had issued an alehouse licence for the Molineux House premises to a William Alfred Brommage, but at the end of the 1895/96 playing season, Brommage indicated his desire to quit the 'licensed trade'. Knowing this, Jack approached the directors of Butlers Brewery in June 1896 with a proposal to become the new landlord of the Molineux Hotel. Although he had no direct experience of running licensed premises, Beatrice certainly had, and her father was still running his pub in the town and would have been on hand if Jack needed any advice or support. In many ways it made sense for Jack and his family to live on the premises at Molineux, where he could be at hand to deal with club-related issues virtually on a twenty-four-hour basis, while at the same time increasing his income and having the benefit of the hotel's much more spacious living accommodation for his growing family. The brewery agreed to Jack's application only on the basis that it was made with the full support of the Wolves board of directors. On 26 June that year, the company secretary of Butlers Brewery (Theodore Addenbrooke, no relation to Jack) wrote to the Wolves board seeking its approval for Jack becoming the manager of Molineux Hotel. The board agreed, and it was Jack himself who wrote the reply to the brewery on behalf of the football club supporting his application. As part of the deal, the brewery took an interest in the club and a representative of Butlers was co-opted into the Wanderers board of directors. (Initially this was Theodore Addenbrooke, who remained a director of the club until the time of First World War. The link between the brewery and the football club remained firm and unbroken for almost a century, until the time Wolves were in severe financial crisis in the 1980s.) So it was that in early July 1896 Jack and Beatrice moved into their new home in the living quarters at the Molineux Hotel, with their two little daughters, Dorothy Beatrice, who had been born in 1893, and her baby sister Olive, who was barely a year old.

For the next four years Jack was busy running both his shop and the hotel, while still undertaking his secretarial duties with the Wolves, for which he received a salary of £100 a year. Sometimes he would be in the rather bizarre position of having to formally write on behalf of the club (in his role as secretary/manager) to himself (in his capacity of hotel manager) over issues such as room availability or refreshments for players. Of course, he would also have to repeat the procedures when he replied to himself, but it is unlikely he would have seen anything odd in this. Jack was a consummate professional in organisational matters, and he would have been at pains to keep stringent records of all his dealings irrespective of which role he was undertaking.

Initially, Jack's tenure at the hotel seems to have been a successful venture. Beatrice took on the role of housekeeper and cook at the hotel, while the children were looked after by a live-in nanny called Lottie Humphries. Beatrice's roast dinners became something of a legend among the players. In 1897 it was written of the Wolves:

The men are in good trim, due to Albert Fletcher (the former player who had become club trainer the previous year) and Charlie Booth, and perhaps, to the joints that Mrs Addenbrooke provides for those players who cannot well get home.

The period of Jack's tenancy at the Molineux Hotel was one of mixed fortunes for the Wanderers club. The financial crisis that had been evident for some time intensified, mainly due to expenditure increasing at a time of falling gates at Molineux. This is highlighted by the fact that gate receipts fell from £3,645 in 1893 to only £2,592 a mere two years later, representing a drop of almost 30 per cent in income. At the annual general meeting of shareholders in 1895, serious concern was expressed over paying wages to full-time professional players during the closed season, and extreme austerity measures, such as abandoning the club's training programme, were advocated. After all, it was said, all the players had to do was keep fit, and employing a trainer to tell them how to do that was nothing more than extravagance. There was conflict between players and the club owners in other areas as well. At the end of the 1893/94 playing season, the directors had summarily sacked the first-team goalkeeper, William Crispin Rose. 'Billy' Rose was a Londoner by birth and had not only played for the great Preston North End club, but had also received international recognition, gaining five caps for England between 1884 and 1891. He had been one of the founding players of Small Heath (later Birmingham City) Football Club, and as he still lived in the Midlands, he was brought in to replace Jack Baynton after he had left Wolves in 1889. Rose had been in goal when Wolves won the cup at Fallowfield in 1893, and his robust, no-nonsense style made him very popular with the crowds. However, he fell from favour with the directors of the club when he circulated a letter amongst his teammates advocating the formation of a trade union for players. Such a suggestion was anathema to the Wolves board, which consisted almost entirely of businessmen and members of the local Conservative Party. A poor season ensued and the club was obliged by disgruntled supporters to undertake an embarrassing climb-down and re-employ Rose a year later. During 1895/96 the relationship between the board and Wolves players continued to be fractious at times. At the beginning of the New Year, three players (including composer Edward Elgar's favourite player, Billy Malpass) were suspended for 'not taking their duties seriously enough'. This came shortly after the club had been forced to close the Molineux for two weeks by the Football Association as a punishment for disturbances in a home match against Everton.

It seemed the season would only be remembered for internal conflict and crisis at the club, but events proved otherwise. Despite a poor League campaign, (finally achieving only fourteenth place of the sixteen teams of the First Division of the time), Wolverhampton Wanderers managed to get to the FA Cup final for the second time in three years. This outstanding feat was achieved to a large extent through the efforts of Billy Malpass, Dick Baugh senior and the captain, Harry Wood, who had played in the 1893 final and gained a second England cap that same season. A valuable contribution to successfully reaching the final against the team from Sheffield, who were simply referred to as 'the Wednesday' had been made by a forward named Billy Beats. Beats was a builder's labourer from the Potteries, and had played for Port Vale as a semi-professional. Wolves' players committee had recommended Beats to the board, and with their approval Jack Addenbrooke had been sent to approach him secure his signature for the Wanderers. Jack found him at work mending a chapel roof in Burslem. Initially Beats was reluctant to join Wolves, but Addenbrooke refused to let him down the ladder to ground level until he changed his mind. Eventually Jack's persistence paid off and Beats capitulated. In accepting a guinea from Jack as a signing-on fee and putting his signature on the forms, Beats duly became a Wolves player.

By this time Jack Addenbrooke had gained a reputation as a canny negotiator when attempting to sign players for Wolves at the 'right price'. In 1892, while playing for the local shopkeepers in a Wolverhampton Cup fixture, eighteen-year-old Joseph Butcher was 'spotted' by Charlie Booth (a former Wolves player and trainer) who was refereeing the game. After the match Joe Butcher was taken to see Jack Addenbrooke, who offered him 7s 6d a week to sign for Wolves. Butcher refused, but the following week was watched by the Harry Allen, the Wolves' captain, while playing in a game held at Molineux Grounds. Having had an outstanding game and scoring, Allan took him again to see Addenbrooke who increased the offer to 10s a week if Joe signed for the Wanderers. Again Butcher refused, but when Allen watched him again in the Wolverhampton Cup final, where he scored five goals, he finally agreed to join Wolves for 15s a week. Despite Butcher having joined the Wolves on a vastly improved wage, Addenbrooke had still gained a prolific marksman at a bargain price. Aware of other clubs' interest in Joe Butcher, Addenbrooke had instructed Harry Allen to bring him to the Molineux Hotel to sign for Wolves by a 'roundabout route', thus avoiding other club representatives who wanted to speak to Butcher. Blackburn Rovers were particularly annoyed by this ruse, as their agent was looking for Joe after the Wolverhampton Cup final and was prepared to offer him over twice as much as Wolves had! Joe Butcher played only three seasons for Wolves before injury ended his career at the age of just twenty-one. He had scored thirty-one goals in seventy-six matches, and had been picked as an England reserve, but was never selected for a full international cap. Butcher had the unique distinction of being the only player in the 1893 FA Cup-winning team to have been born in Wolverhampton, and in later life became the full-time secretary of the local branch of the National Union of Sheet Metal Workers & Braziers.

The cup final of 1896 was the third one the Wanderers had been in with Addenbrooke acting as secretary-manager, and it was held at the Crystal Palace in London, close to the building of the same name. It was only the second time the final had been held there, but it was considered a suitable venue because of the large number of spectators it could hold. At the final, Wolves were at a disadvantage when Billy Rose ruled himself out through injury and his place in goal was taken by a fairly inexperienced amateur 'keeper from Willenhall named Tennant. Wednesday, on the other hand, had many experienced FA Cup players, having been semi-finalists in the competition in the two previous seasons.

The game took place on 18 April, and unsurprisingly Wolves went behind after just a few minutes' play when Spikesley of Wednesday found the net. Wolves equalised less than ten minutes later through David Black. The Wanderers fell behind again when Spikesley got a second and decisive goal against the Wolves. Tennant had been injured in the build up to this second goal, and was dazed and unsighted when the ball had crossed his goal line and had bounced back out. At the end of the match, he asked Jack Earp (the Wednesday captain) when the replay was to be, as he genuinely thought the game had been drawn. Earp replied triumphantly, 'There is no replay old man! We won by two goals to one as you will see when we take the medals!' 'But how,' a confused Tennant responded, 'for only one shot passed me!' (Writing in the *Sporting Star* over thirty years later, Dick Baugh recalled Spikesley's second goal as being at least 17 yards offside!) Added to the fact that he believed a perfectly good second goal from Black had been disallowed by the referee, it is easy to understand why he felt Wolves had been 'robbed'. It was a belief that stayed with him and rankled for the remainder of his life. Joe Butcher, on the other hand, always believed Wolves' defeat was entirely their own making. The team's training schedule for the final had included a walk to Rugeley and back – some 32 miles in all. Many players were so exhausted by the ordeal that they sought overnight accommodation in public houses and inns on the return journey. Joe believed the players were still recovering from fatigue when they played in the final.

During the next three seasons, Wolves were unable to repeat such a good cup run, but their League performance was steady and reasonably good. In each of the playing seasons between 1896 and 1900 they won fourteen of their League games and on one occasion were placed as high as third in the table, but major problems still existed behind the scenes at Molineux. By 1900, the Wolves were on the verge of bankruptcy. The directors had to let the better players such as Billy Beats and Harry Wood leave the club because they could not afford the £4 weekly wage for each man. At the start of the 1900/01 season, Wolves only had twenty-five professional players on the books, and most of these had been signed from local minor clubs such as Willenhall Pickwick. The season also witnessed the start of a decline that nearly resulted in Wanderers going out of business. Within a year they were operating at a deficit of over £1,300, and a poor response from an appeal to the public for funding meant club president Alfred Hickman had to put his hand deep into his pocket to keep the creditors and bailiffs away from the doors of Molineux.

With the reduction in funding and the change in circumstances, Wolves' hierarchy ordered significant changes in the managerial structure at the club, and these greatly affected Addenbrooke's role. The 'selection committee' – on which club founder John Brodie still served – was disbanded, and its duties of recruitment and retention of players, as well as team selection, were taken on by Addenbrooke. This made his role as manager one that followers of the modern game would readily recognise. The accompanying increase in his workload for the Wolves meant that Jack's continued tenure at the Molineux Hotel would have become increasingly onerous, and by the end of the year he had surrendered the licence of the hostelry and moved his family out of the premises.

There was another, much more personal reason why the Addenbrookes left Molineux Hotel at the end of that first year of the new century. In the June of that year their youngest daughter Olive was struck down by the viral illness scarlatina. Though often seen as identical to scarlet fever, scarlatina was in fact a less acute form of the disease, but could be just as serious nonetheless. In the days before antibiotics were readily available, scarlatina mainly affected children between the ages of four and eight. After the age of ten years most children had acquired natural protective antibodies, and scarlet fever at this age or older was rare. Young Olive was only six years old, and had been taken ill with a high temperature and fever when the family doctor was sent for. Dr Quinn from nearby Stafford Street was unwell himself at this time with a severe cold, so a locum named Dr Green from Birmingham attended the poorly child. With no known cure at the time, the little girl slipped into a coma and, in the presence of a distraught Jack and Beatrice, passed away three days later, on 27 June 1900. With the old hotel holding such sad and tragic memories, Jack and his family had no qualms in moving to the living quarters above the tobacconist shop he had acquired at No. 60 Dudley Street.

The sadness felt by Jack and Beatrice at the loss of their youngest child must have been deeply felt, but may have been lessened a little a couple of years later when Beatrice gave birth to a fine baby son. Named after his father and bearing his mother's maiden name, John Hibell Addenbrooke was born in 1902. With the new baby, and daughter Dorothy almost ten years older, the family found the living accommodation in Dudley Street increasingly cramped. The need for more space was exacerbated when Beatrice gave birth to another daughter, Marjorie, in the summer of 1904. Although he bought the freehold on the shop in Dudley Street in September 1915, Jack moved his family into rented accommodation very close to Molineux Grounds sometime around 1906. The family stayed at No. 45 Waterloo Road for five years, before moving to No. 11 Paget Road in Tettenhall. During the latter years of the First World War, Jack moved yet again to a fine three-storey terraced house on Wolverhampton's prestigious Tettenhall Road, and it was at No. 26 that he was to remain until his untimely death in 1922. (In July 1918, at the age of twenty-five, Dorothy married John Jones, an engineer who lived in North Street. Shortly afterwards, like John Brodie's eldest son before them, they emigrated to start a new life in Canada.)

Despite the ongoing problems at the Molineux, Jack continued to enjoy a good reputation and high status within the business community of Wolverhampton during the early years of the twentieth century. He had become the secretary of the Wolverhampton Charity Association, an umbrella organisation that co-ordinated charitable and fundraising activities in the town. In 1901, like many of his fellow traders, he was asked to stand as a guarantor for a proposed exhibition that was to be held in Wolverhampton the following year. Industrial and artistic exhibitions had been popular in Britain since the Great Exhibition of 1851, and a very successful Art & Industry Exhibition had been held at Molineux House and grounds in 1869. Located in the West Park, Wolverhampton's Exhibition of 1902 would be a showcase to the world of locally made items, as well as national and internationally produced goods. Visitors would bring trade to the town and shopkeepers like Jack Addenbrooke would benefit. Yet even though it had Royal approval and was opened by the Duke of Connaught (Edward VII's brother), the exhibition was not a financial success and lost £30,000. As a guarantor of the venture, Jack would have had to forfeit the £5 he had deposited with the organisers when the loss was declared, and not surprisingly failed to support suggestions for a new exhibition the following year. By the end of the 1905/06 season, the enduring financial situation and lack of investment in the club resulted in the inevitable, and Wolves were relegated for the first time in their history. After being subjected to some real thrashings at Newcastle (8-0) and Sunderland (7-2), Wolves finished the season in bottom place with only twenty-three points and having lost twenty-seven of their thirty-eight matches. They were not to regain their top-flight position for some twenty-six years!

Life in the Second Division became fairly humdrum for Wanderers, and a mid-table place in the second tier was all they seemed to aspire to. Local interest waned, gates fell and the quality of the team suffered, but the spirit of Wolves never died, as the remarkable events of 1907/08 were to show. The financial crisis at the club had become something of a permanent fixture, and with Wolverhampton Wanderers languishing mid-table in the Second Division, Addenbrooke was again looking for local (and preferably cheap) options to fill the ranks of the first team. He was lucky to find an amateur, locally based player who was to gain iconic status as a Wolves player in the final years of Edwardian England. The player was Kenneth Reginald Gunnery Hunt.

Although not a native of Wolverhampton, Kenneth Hunt had lived in the town since the turn of the century and had been educated at the local grammar school. He was the son of the vicar of St Mark's church in Chapel Ash, just a short distance from Molineux Grounds. Although a fine cricketer, Hunt excelled at football at school and later at Oxford University where he had gained 'Blues' and had played for the famous Corinthians. He gained a reputation as a hard and determined half-back. Kenneth Hunt had started playing for the Wolves on a part-time basis at the start of the 1907/08 season, while he attended Queen's College, Oxford, where he was studying divinity with the aim of following his father into the Church. Addenbrooke was undoubtedly very glad to be able to avail himself of the services of the very fit and keen undergraduate, who would only accept travelling expenses, so as not to jeopardise his amateur status. In spite of his acquisition, Wolves were always in a very precarious position financially, and by Christmas 1907 the town's evening paper, the *Express & Star*, was so concerned about the club's plight that it offered financial assistance for the purchase of players. Thus, the availability of someone of Hunt's experience must have seemed like a godsend to the Wolves board. Hunt would finish his studies on a Friday afternoon and make his way by train to Wolverhampton. After spending the night at his parents' home in Chapel Ash, he would be available for team selection by Addenbrooke on the afternoon of the following day.

Along with Hunt, Addenbrooke had assembled a team of local men and one or two more experienced players from further afield. Among the former were team captain Billy Wooldridge from Netherton, near Dudley, and Jack Sheldon from Wolverhampton, who was later to die in battle on the Western Front in 1918. The attack was led by a tough old north-easterner named George Hedley, who had previously lifted the trophy in 1902 while playing for Sheffield United.

Against all the odds, Wolves reached the final in 1908 by winning their matches in the preceding rounds by narrow margins. In the tie against Swindon earlier in the year, Kenneth Hunt had come on for Wooldridge, the Wolves skipper, who had been injured. In true heroic style, he changed the run of play, and helped Wolves snatch a victory, even though he was knocked unconscious twice in the course of the match. The three cup games prior to the final were not so dramatic for Wolves, but they were very close-run things. The team scored only seven goals, whereas their opponents in the final, Newcastle, had hit the net no fewer than eighteen times in the corresponding ties. In sharp contrast to Wolves, Newcastle at the time was 'riding on the crest of a wave'. They were one of the most successful clubs in the history of the game before the First World War. They were the previous season's champions and had reached the cup final no less than four times in the seven seasons between 1904 and 1911.

Training for the final seems to have been a rather leisurely affair for the Wanderers players compared with the rigours a present-day team would endure. They did some work to develop their ball skills, but trainer Albert Fletcher also organised long healthy walks in the countryside around Matlock, where the team were staying for a week prior to the final, which the players undertook while dressed in three-piece suits and flat caps! These ramblings were neither as long nor as onerous as the 'route march' to Rugeley endured by the FA Cup finalists in 1897.

It says a lot about team morale that Addenbrooke had engendered at the time that even though Kenneth Hunt had been selected to play for the England team against Wales in April of 1908, he forewent that honour in order to turn out for Wolverhampton Wanderers in the cup final. His teammate Billy Harrison's wife was in the latter stages of pregnancy and actually delivered triplets on the day of the final. Billy was unperturbed by events at home and still played in the match! As might be expected, the Geordies' confidence was sky-high prior to the final, and the club requested permission to have the team photographed with the cup before the final had even taken place. In the light of subsequent events, there must have been many Magpie supporters who were eternally grateful that the request was refused. This confidence in a predicted Newcastle victory was not felt on Tyneside alone. Despite parochial and partisan emotions felt by people in Wolverhampton, neutral pundits had little doubt as to the outcome of the thirty-fifth annual cup competition. Addenbrooke's Wolves were described in the London press as a 'rough-and-tumble team', and sharp contrasts were made with the smooth and silky skills of the Newcastle side they would meet at the Crystal Palace (the ground that had been used to stage the final of the competition since 1895). On the morning of the game, *Sporting Life* declared, 'There is no comparison on paper. Newcastle should win in handsome style.'

Not surprisingly, 'cup fever' had gradually built up in Wolverhampton as the Wanderers had progressed through the various stages of the competition and the final approached. The main local newspaper planned to utilise the technological advances of the day to bring details of the final to Wulfrunians as quickly as possible. The directors of the *Express & Star* stated that they were willing to personally bear the expense of having a new-fangled telephone line installed between a small wooden hut in the Crystal Palace ground and their Queen Street offices. Costing 45s per hour, the telephone would be used by a correspondent at the match to transmit the score at regular intervals to the newspaper office in Wolverhampton. This would be conveyed to the crowd assembled in Queen Street by being chalked up on a large blackboard, which was to be suspended out of an upper-floor window for all to see. Other commercial interests also used the occasion for topical publicity, and readers of local papers were assured by advertisers that the winner would be the one whose players invested a 'lucky sixpence' to purchase their cocoa! The Oxo company also exploited the interest in the cup by putting on a competition in the local papers. The prize for the several lucky winners was to be 'a free trip to London and back, with reserved and numbered 5s seats at the Palace'.

With all preparations completed, the legion of Wolves supporters made their way towards the metropolis on the many 'special' trains that had been laid on for the purpose. With the exception of the fortunate winners of the Oxo competition, the total cost of the day's outing, including transport and admission price, would have been very nearly the equivalent of an industrial worker's weekly wage at the time. However, few true supporters would have let that stop them going to the game, especially as there was so little chance of League success in the near future.

Greeting their many excited supporters at Wolverhampton Low Level station on the morning of 25 April, team members happily posed for photographs. Addenbrooke had specially commissioned a London & North Western Railway Company train, pulled by an engine named *Messenger*, to take the team to the final. It had been decorated with flags and bunting, and a sign declaring to all and sundry, 'Here come the Wolves!' Upon reaching the capital, supporters from both sides joined Jack Addenbrooke, the club directors and the team at a divine service at St Paul's Cathedral, undoubtedly all praying for 'the right result'. Afterwards the crowds made their way to the Crystal Palace for the game. The weather had been very poor and totally out of keeping with the time of year. Snow had caused the cancellation of games at Southampton and Reading, and conditions at the Crystal Palace ground were described as 'rain in torrents and pitilessly driven sleet, alternated with heavy snow showers'. However, just prior to kick-off the stormy skies cleared and the threatening clouds were replaced by bright sunshine.

Watched by less than 75,000 (the smallest crowd for several years), the game kicked off at the appointed time under the control of referee Mr T. P. Campbell. The heavy weather had made the embankments slippery for spectators, but this did not stop one Wolves fan from appearing in a homemade fur wolf-suit. Despite the effect being somewhat spoilt by the lack of a mask, and the wearer insisting on retaining his flat cap, many must have envied his outfit on such a cold day! Others at the game included both the mayors of Wolverhampton and Newcastle – Sir Alfred Hickman (the Wanderers' president), and the famous politician A. J. Balfour (leader of the Conservative Party and one-time Prime Minister of Great Britain).

The initial play heralded dire warnings for the Wanderers. Skill and training gave way to nervousness and uncertainty. Newcastle, by far the more composed side, mounted several early attacks. As if overawed by the big occasion, Wolves allowed gaps to develop between the forwards and the half-backs, and these were duly exploited by the Tynesiders. At the other end of the park, Wolves attackers Pedley and Radford had their efforts thwarted by the Newcastle international defender Gardner on several occasions. The other Wolves forward, Hedley, either slipped or failed to put in a proper shot when in front of goal, even though he had already completed a lot of hard work in receiving long passes and getting the ball under control. There was a tendency for the Wolves attackers to try and 'walk' the ball into the net, but considering the Newcastle team's skill and experience this type of play would always be fruitless. Something dramatic was needed to break the deadlock and lift the Wolves.

'Cometh the hour, cometh the man' is an old adage, but never more true when recalling Kenneth Hunt's actions on that day. After nearly forty minutes, a feeble and messy scramble in the Newcastle goalmouth saw the ball cleared by a defender's long kick. It was intercepted by the Oxford undergraduate, who was standing some 40 yards upfield. Calmly and thoughtfully, Hunt struck the ball back towards the opposition's goal with such ferocity that the Magpies' goalkeeper could do nothing but embarrassingly palm the ball into his own net. Wolves were one up! Hunt's goal has been described as 'speculative' and even 'lucky' by analysts who reason that he was not a proven or regular goalscorer and was not in the habit of trying long-range shots. There may be some truth in this, as it was the only goal he scored for Wolves that season. His reason for trying a shot will never be known, but more important was the effect that it had on the rest of the Wolves players. The team suddenly believed in itself, and the vague possibility of a win became an almost certainty as the Wolves piled on the pressure. Whereas before Hunt's goal almost nothing had seemed to go right, now the Wanderers could hardly put a foot wrong. They hustled, bustled, jockeyed their foes and fought for every ball, grasping at half-chances at every opportunity in a style reminiscent of much earlier times. Newcastle was taken aback at this newfound dynamism from the team that they had so recently dismissed as no-hopers, and were at a loss at how to handle the Wolves' determination and aggression. Hunt himself led the way in maintaining the pressure. His speed and power were phenomenal, and Wilson, one of the Geordies who was detailed to mark him, ended up 'doing the splits' while attempting to catch Hunt, who was running with the ball. The Molineux men went further ahead in the second half through Hedley and Harrison, before exertion and strain started to take their toll. Newcastle managed to score in the dying minutes of the game through Howie, but by then it was far too late for the Magpies to salvage anything more than a little pride from a game that they expected to win easily.

The final whistle was greeted by scenes of wild excitement on the Crystal Palace terraces. Wolves supporters cheered themselves hoarse as the Lord Mayor of London, Sir Henry Bell, handed the trophy to Wooldridge, the Wolves skipper, who boastfully declared to loud applause that it would not be the last time that he would have the honour of receiving it (sadly it was). Newcastle took their surprising defeat in good part as W. Hudson, MP for Central Newcastle, gave an impromptu speech in which he congratulated the Wanderers. Although unexpected, Wolves' victory was very popular in various parts of the country. At a match on Merseyside between Everton and Sheffield Wednesday (the finalists from the previous year), the underdogs' victory was greeted with great cheers.

The news of Wolves' success was greeted in Wolverhampton with jubilation, especially outside the *Express & Star* offices in Queen Street, where crowds had been arriving by tram all afternoon to hear reports on their team's progress. Spotted among the crowd was the Revd Robert Hunt, Kenneth's father, who was as keen as anyone was to hear the news from London. In what was considered an outlandish display of fanaticism for the victorious team, a resident of Park Village devised a flag in Wolves' colours and hoisted it up outside his house. At Dudley and West Bromwich, the news caused crowds to congregate on the streets to excitedly discuss the victory.

In true sporting spirit, the Wolves board received a congratulatory telegraph from West Bromwich Albion, which was duly published in the local press. Other local reactions to the victory were somewhat strange. In a letter to the editor of the *Express & Star* one correspondent advocated a change in Wolves colours away from the 'dowdy and dull gold and black' back to the more cheerful red of bygone days, which, he argued, would be more fitting for a winning side.

The success of Wolverhampton Wanderers in the cup final of 1908 marked a high point in the history of the club up until that time. The cup had only been won once before by a club from the Second Division, but never by one as low down in the rankings as Wolves were then. The cup run had brought a very welcome £3,000 into the coffers at Molineux and this probably staved off the threat of bankruptcy (until after the First World War at least). In Kenneth Hunt, Addenbrooke had discovered the first really iconic hero for Wolves' supporters to admire and praise since the days of John Brodie. 'Kenny' Hunt, as he became known, brought more honour to the club and the town by being selected for the successful Great Britain football team in the London Olympic competition later that year. Despite only playing one more complete season in Wolverhampton's old gold and black, the relationship between Kenneth Hunt and the town remained strong for many years. In 1920, when he was well into his late thirties, 15,000 turned up at Molineux to watch him play in a friendly against Notts County. He reciprocated the loyalty later when he chose the colours for Grindal House at Highgate School in London where he taught. Even today, boys from that house still play their sporting fixtures in Hunt's beloved gold and black!

For Jack Addenbrooke himself, the unexpected success of 1908 secured his position at the club effectively for the rest of his life. Even though directors then were not as ready to dismiss officials for poor team performance as their modern counterparts might be, Jack's position must surely have been come under threat as Wolves continued to underperform thereafter. Instead, thanks to the cup triumph he was the toast of the town, and the recipient of a fine gold medal from a grateful club to thank him for his efforts.

The following years brought little in the way of further success to the Wanderers, although, only a season after the triumph at the Crystal Palace, Jack Addenbrooke was again the recipient of an award because of his work in the world of football. In June 1909, along with his friend and opposite number at Aston Villa George Ramsey, he was awarded a long-service medal and illuminated address by the Football League in recognition of twenty-one years' service with the organisation. This, together with his service to the Staffordshire County Football Association, of which he was one time vice-president and committee member since 1894, ensured Wolverhampton Wanderers were always well represented at meetings of the sport's governing bodies.

As the century progressed into its second decade, war loomed in Europe, and even though Wanderers were unable to repeat the heroics of 1908, they had started to make some progress in the League. In 1914, in the last full season before hostilities commenced, they had again finished mid-table in Division Two, but some felt they were making steady progress and with a bit of luck promotion would eventually come. However, the war was to stop all this and long-term plans at Molineux were put on hold. Despite staggering through a meaningless final season into 1915, which ended in Wolves finishing fourth in the Second Division, football had become very unpopular among the general public because players had not been released by their clubs to join the armed forces. Directors at Wolves, like many of their counterparts at other large football clubs, argued that since most people believed 'it would be all over by Christmas' the players would be demobbed before they had chance to serve at the front. They also argued that continuing football would maintain public morale and matches could be a useful venue for recruiting sergeants to get more young men to volunteer for active service. However, as the war entered its second year, such arguments held little water and the Football Association ordered the suspension of all competitions. Most players on Wolves' books left the club to work in local engineering factories, which were fully engaged in making war materials and munitions.

As the war dragged on, Jack was involved in organising a much watered-down football programme consisting in the main part of friendly matches played for raising funds for Army charities. Molineux played host to a match involving an Army XI, and Kenneth Hunt is known to have played in a charity match in 1916. Almost in the role of caretaker, Jack oversaw the use of the pitch as a training ground for local militia during the hostilities, but he dropped straight back into his old routine when football recommenced in 1919.

Despite a couple of new faces in the Wanderers line-up in the first post-war season, eight of the regular team had played for Wolves before the war and two of them had played in the cup final of 1908. Not surprisingly, the team got off to a poor start. The season was marred by crowd trouble and Wolves were knocked out of the second round of the cup at home to Cardiff and finished nineteenth in Division Two. The League performances the following season were little better, although in an FA Cup run reminiscent of 1908, Wolves made it to the final. At one of the last FA Cup finals played before the opening of the Empire Stadium at Wembley, Wolves met Tottenham Hotspur at Chelsea's ground, Stamford Bridge. It was the fourth time that Jack had taken a Wolves team to the final, but it was the first time they had met a side from London.

The match took place on St George's Day, 23 April 1921, and the guest of honour was the King. The two teams were presented to King George V, and Wolves' new skipper Val Gregory introduced the team. In May 1920, Gregory joined Wolverhampton Wanderers from Watford on Jack Addenbrooke's recommendation for a record transfer fee of £1,500. He had made forty-three wartime appearances for Watford of the Southern League, and had also made guest appearances for Arsenal. He was destined to spend the remainder of his professional career at Wolves, making his final appearances for the team in the 1922/23 season that saw the club relegated to the Third Division. He became a player-coach in 1925, and finished his playing days as an amateur for Butler Sports & Football Club. He finally ended his service as a coach at Molineux in 1938 due to ill health.

The inferior quality of the Wolves' line-up was exposed time and again and their play was described as 'disjointed', although they reached half-time without conceding a goal. From the kick-off spectators could see the game was going to be a poor one, as torrential rain soon turned the pitch into a quagmire. Any Wolves supporter hoping for a repeat of 1908 was to be sorely disappointed, as players slipped and slid all over the pitch. In front of a crowd of 74,000, many of whom had spilled over onto the running track around the pitch to get a better view, Spurs had the better of the first half but were denied by Wolves' giant 'keeper Noel George. Frank (Noel) George had been born in Lichfield on 28 December 1897, and had played local football before joining Wolverhampton Wanderers along with Val Gregory in 1920. He was diagnosed as being terminally ill with a disease of the gums and died in 1929, having played in 292 games for Wolves. His manager at the time, Frank Buckley, was convinced that George's death was due to ill-fitting dentures, and from that time on ensured that all his players who wore dentures were examined by a dentist every six months.

The second half continued in the same vein, and within ten minutes the Wanderers' defences were finally and perhaps inevitably breached. The scorer was a twenty-year-old winger called Jimmy Dimmock, who struck the ball into the back of the net from a good 20 yards out after it had rebounded off a Wolves defender named Woodward. Spurs had the chance of a second goal just minutes later, when Bert Bliss shot just wide from a free kick. Wolves tried hard and almost equalised late in the game, but it was not to be. The final score was 1-0.

The excitement of the cup competition soon died away and the following season (1921/22) saw Wolves revert back to their same old pedestrian ways, winning only thirteen of their forty-two League fixtures and being knocked out of the cup at home in the first round by Preston North End. However, the season was to be remembered for a much sadder reason than team performances. It was to be Jack's last in charge of the Wanderers.

As the season ended, Jack began to complain of feeling unwell, and his usual flair and enthusiasm for managing the Wolves was noticeably lacking. Increasingly suffering from severe headaches and breathing difficulties, he took time off from his duties in June on the advice of his friend and neighbour, club physician Richard Wolverson. Despite the rest, Jack's health did not improve, and on the 25 July Dr Wolverson addressed a board meeting of the club's directors and gave them a prognosis of Jack's condition. It was unanimously agreed to grant Addenbrooke a six-month leave of absence on full pay, and a letter of sympathy was forwarded to Beatrice concerning Jack's illness. In the meanwhile, his duties were be taken on by a former Wanderers player from Tettenhall named Albert Hoskins.

All through August, Jack's health continued to deteriorate, and in the first week of September he was taken into the town's Royal Hospital. It was there that he died on the morning of Thursday 7 September 1922, aged fifty-seven.

Jack Addenbrooke's funeral service took place the following Monday at St Peter's Collegiate church, conducted by the rector, the Revd J. J. G. Stockley. Many townspeople had drawn their blinds or closed their curtains as a sign of respect for the Wolves manager and it was reported that 'a considerable number of people lined the route of the cortège from the residence of the late Mr Addenbrooke'. The church was packed with mourners, chief among which were his wife Beatrice, his son John, and four of his brothers. Board members and old friends from the club such as Tommy Cliff (who had been Wolves' secretary before Jack), Alderman Levi Johnson, Charles Crump and John Brodie were also in attendance, as was Wolverhampton's mayor (James Thompson) and members of the town council. Numerous wreaths and floral tributes were placed on the coffin before it was taken for interment at Jeffcock Road cemetery. Among these were ones from family members, various football clubs and organisations, the Wolverhampton Tobacconists Association, and perhaps saddest of all, one from his daughter 'Dorothy, John and baby' in Vancouver, Canada – a grandchild he had not lived to see.

And so, the youngest of the three Jacks was the first to pass away. But his legacy would be enduring. Jack Addenbrooke had died a wealthy man, leaving nearly £7,500 – a considerable fortune at the time – but he left far more than that. His achievement in guiding Wolverhampton Wanderers from being little more than a local amateur football club to one of national and international renown as a founder member of the world's first Football League and with two FA Cup wins from four final appearances, could hardly ever be matched. In consolidating Wanderers as a top club during nearly forty years of unbroken service, and so contributing greatly to the emergence of Britain's national sport, football fans everywhere should laud the name of 'Jack Addenbrooke'.

Above: Wolves, 1902
The Wolves team at the Molineux Grounds,
pictured with Jack Addenbrooke (*left*).
(WWFC collection)

Left: Jack Addenbrooke
A sketch of Jack Addenbrooke, Wolves'
secretary and manager, *c.* 1888.
(Author's collection)

Above: Molineux Hotel
The Wolves' headquarters, *c.* 1920. (Author's collection)

Right: Jack Addenbrooke
A posed studio shot of Jack Addenbrooke, aged
around thirty, taken in the mid-1890s. (Addenbrooke
family collection)

Left: John Addenbrooke Senior, *c.* 1883
A head-and-shoulders detail from a larger family group photograph. (Addenbrooke family collection)

Below: Jack Addenbrooke
Seen in the back row, third on the right, with other Football League club secretaries in the 1890s.

Above: Jack Addenbrooke, Aged Eighteen
Addenbrooke and his family around 1880.
(Addenbrooke family collection)

Right: Addenbrooke's Tobacconist
A sketch of the frontage of Jack
Addenbrooke's tobacconist's shop in
the High Street (later in Dudley Street).
(Author's collection)

Illuminated Scroll

A colour reproduction of the illuminated scroll presented to John Addenbrooke by the Football League in 1909 to mark twenty-five years of service. (Addenbrooke family collection)

CONCLUSION

Memories of football matches live long in the minds of those who witnessed them. The raw emotions, excitement and passions they evoke can stimulate recollections in ways that cannot easily be explained or shared with others who weren't there. So it is with the Wolves' early games, and we have to read between the lines of the rather dry and factual match reports of the time to imagine what skilful players and exciting matches there might have been. We have no visual record of Brodie, Baynton and their teammates playing and might question if they would have held their own in a modern-day side. Who knows? But it is probably unlikely, when the enormous effects of modern nutritional and training regimes are taken into account.

Thus they might have to be assessed and appreciated in other ways. The three Jacks, and the others, came from normal backgrounds and essentially stayed true to their roots. Unlike many modern footballers, they did not become enormously wealthy, nor lead lives aloof and detached from the community into which they had been born. Football was only one aspect of their lives, albeit a very significant one.

The club they started and worked so hard for waited a long time for the fourth Jack to come along and make up the pack, but it did happen when Sir Jack Hayward (and later Steve Morgan) became involved in the Wolves in recent years to maintain the vision and renew the dream that first emerged from that meeting in Blakenhall in 1876.

So, there were more than just echoes left when the sun finally went down on the lives of the three Jacks and their contemporaries all those years ago. Even though there are very few left now who will remember them personally, they enabled all true supporters to be able to say with conviction, 'We are forever Wolves!'

SOURCES & BIBLIOGRAPHY

The Origins of Wolverhampton Wanderers has been compiled utilising mainly primary source material. Details of the family composition of the central characters of this history have been gleaned from National Census returns, civic records and family knowledge. Information on various local schools has been taken from headmasters' logbooks and other school records for the period concerned. Other primary sources include reports from local newspapers the *Sports Argus* (Birmingham), the *Wolverhampton Chronicle*, the *Express & Star* and its sister publication the *Sporting Star*; articles in Wolverhampton Wanderers' match-day programmes as well as licensing and other public records. These sources, along with others that include illustrations, are stored in public archives at Wolverhampton, Birmingham and Stafford. Other illustrations are acknowledged within the caption texts.

Anecdotal evidence and illustrations have been kindly furnished by descendants of Jack Baynton, Jack Addenbrooke and Wolverhampton Wanderers Football Club.

Some of the works I have drawn on are listed below:

Allman, Geoff, Wolverhampton Wanderers Football Club. (Stroud: Tempus Publishing Ltd, 2002)

Gibbons, Philip, Association Football in Victorian England: A History of the Game from 1863 to 1900. (Leicestershire: Upfront Publishing, 2002)

Golesworthy, Maurice, The Encyclopedia of Association Football, eighth edition. (London: Robert Hale Ltd, 1967)

Hendley, John, Wolves On This Day: History, Facts and Figures from Every day of the Year. (Brighton: Pitch Publishing Ltd, 2009)

Mander, Gerald P. & Norman W. Tildesley, History of Wolverhampton. (Wolverhampton CB Corporation, 1906)

Mason, Frank, The Book of Wolverhampton: The Story of an Industrial Town. (London: Barracuda Books Ltd, 1979)

Matthews, Tony, Wolverhampton Wanderers: The Complete Record. (Derby: Breedon Books, 2008)

Quirke, Patrick A., Molineux House: A History. (Wolverhampton: Wolverhampton Archives and Local Studies, 2009)

Smart, John Blythe, The WOW Factor: A Concise History of Early Soccer and the Men Who Made It. (Blythe Smart Publications, 2003)

Upton, Chris, A History of Wolverhampton. (Stroud: The History Press, 2007)

Young, Percy M., The Wolves: The First Eighty Years. (London: Stanley Paul & Co., 1959)

SECRET
HASTINGS &
ST LEONARDS

Tina Brown

AMBERLEY

To my dear friends Villi, Momo, Luidmil and Momchil.
I hope one day you can visit these magical places.

First published 2018

Amberley Publishing
The Hill, Stroud
Gloucestershire, GL5 4EP

www.amberley-books.com

Copyright © Tina Brown, 2018

The right of Tina Brown to be identified as the
Author of this work has been asserted in accordance
with the Copyrights, Designs and Patents Act 1988.

ISBN 978 1 4456 7987 7 (print)
ISBN 978 1 4456 7988 4 (ebook)

British Library Cataloguing in Publication Data.
A catalogue record for this book is available from the
British Library.

Origination by Amberley Publishing.
Printed in Great Britain.

Contents

Introduction

The definition of the word 'secret' is something unknown or hidden, a skeleton in the cupboard, something that was once commonly known but is now an intriguing piece of information; it is a mystery or something undercover or underground that few know about. With that in mind, welcome to *Secret Hastings & St Leonards*, and to a journey to discover the lesser-known people, places and events that have helped shape Hastings into the town we know today.

Hastings has long been one of the most popular seaside towns on the south-east coast. It sees thousands of people emerge onto its streets for bank holidays and throughout the year at the numerous festivals and events the town has become famous for. But when one thinks of Hastings there are probably a couple of famous things that spring to mind: Hastings Castle and the Battle of Hastings. Although these were significant in shaping both the history of the town and country, there are other events and people who have also played an important role in the town's past.

The Hastings area, encompassing Hastings' old town, Burton St Leonards, Bexhill, Rye and the surrounding villages, has a rich and varied history. The area offers vibrant contrasts, from the quaint streets and passageways of the old town and Rye to the elegant resorts of Burton St Leonards and Bexhill and the rural charm of outlying villages, each being unique in character, architecture and atmosphere.

As someone who was born and brought up in Hastings, I feel very attached to the town and maybe this is why I feel so at home showing people around as part of my guided tours business, which sees hundreds of visitors each year eager to learn about unusual snippets of historical information.

Hastings is a unique place steeped in history, though sadly some of it is forgotten and seldom talked about. As part of my work I meet people from all over the world and am able to show them the secrets that the old town has to offer. I also meet many locals who often tell me that the information I give them and the places I take them to they never knew existed. Throughout this book I will share many of those places, histories and also people connected to the town who have been forgotten about. As you turn the pages of this book the past will be brought back to life and secrets will be revealed.

Every year I am told new snippets of historical information and carry out extensive research into the town's past to include in my tours and also in my writing projects, of which there are many. I hope you will find this ensemble of tales interesting and perhaps a little mysterious too. But above all it is hoped that after reading about the secrets the area has to offer, you will look at the town in a different light. Look beyond the obvious and ask questions, and you will most certainly be rewarded.

As you walk around, look up and you will see old objects all around you, like this old clock located on Hendy Home Store, High Street.

1. Fishing and Maritime Heritage

Today, Hastings and this part of the Sussex coast is known for seafood and fishing, a long-standing tradition within this unique community. When you ask anyone who has fond memories of the town, they always mention the fishing boats and beaches. Visitors travel from miles around to purchase and take home the delicious fish caught off the coast of Hastings. The fishermen have long been a part of the town, and it is hoped they always will be.

Ancient Harbour

It can only be imagined what the town must have looked like when it had an ancient harbour. Many forget its importance in this respect. This part of the coast is exposed to the full force of the south-west winds and by the end of the twelfth century the eastward drift along the shore was starting to make access in and out of the town's harbour difficult, which resulted in much trade being lost to Rye and Winchelsea. The town was able to provide twenty-one ships to the fleet of the Cinque Ports during the thirteenth century, but just 100 years later they could only provide three; by the late 1400s what had once been a thriving harbour and port was a small fishing village. There were many attempts to try and regain the town's harbour, but many were fruitless due to the strong elements and currents.

In 1595 another attempt began to construct the harbour. A great deal of money was put into the project and local labour was sought – it was stated that all men may be called upon to go and work. Much satisfactory work was achieved over the time, however this was also short-lived due to the conditions of the weather and other unpredictable factors that were out of everyone's control. In the years 1611, 1613, 1618 and 1621, among others, work was commenced only to be brought to a stop once more. In 1656, a severe storm took away the remains of the pier.

DID YOU KNOW?
Few Hastings fishermen are known by their true names, each having a nickname linked with their skill or family. Bones was a nickname of the Willis family of fishermen and Snatcher was a nickname given to the Swaine family of fishermen.

So, what happened next with the plans to rebuild the harbour? By the end of the eighteenth century Hastings was starting a new part of its life – the birth of the new seaside resort – and its population was improving greatly. There were thoughts at this point to try and increase the prosperity of the town further with plans again for the construction of a harbour. In 1828 a gentleman by the name of John Rennie looked to start a new venture; however little is documented about this attempt, only that his suggestions were noted to have been far too ambitious. There were several other plans and ideas submitted, including those by Mr James Burton, who designed Burton St Leonards and also included a harbour in his plans in the area that is today known as St Leonards.

The year 1838 saw two further plans submitted to the then Harbour Committee for consideration. Both plans were to build opposite the fish market. One was submitted by Lieutenant Colonel S. W. Williams and would contain 24 acres at high tide, with a landing pier in the centre. Stone could be used from the nearby East Hill cliffs for the construction. The other plan was from Mr John Smith, a Hastings stonemason and a member of the Harbour Committee. In it he used an old pier and shelter rocks on which to base the harbour arm. Mr Smith's design was much smaller and would be 7 acres with an inner harbour of 3 acres. Colonel Williams' design was eventually selected and the council decided that it should be constructed as part of a borough improvement and an act should be applied for to carry it out. After much discussion the project was dropped after little support or financial assistance from the government; however, Colonel Williams was presented with a fine silver inkstand in honour of the town's appreciation for his efforts.

There have been many documented shipwrecks off this stretch of the coast and one report from Christmas 1838 shows the need for a harbour:

> The beautifully clear and frosty weather which we enjoyed on Christmas Day was continued till noon on Wednesday, when the wind suddenly changed from the north to the south west and continued to augment in violence until dusk, at which period the squalls were truly terrific.
>
> Thousands were assembled as spectators of the awfully terrific sight of four vessels dashing to pieces upon the beach

In 1889 another attempt was made to build a harbour. It was very nearly successful too; however, despite initial approval funds soon ran low, and all that remains today is the arm of the harbour projecting out into the sea. The arm was damaged in 1910 and then again in more recent times.

Occasionally, onlookers are treated to a secret that is buried out at sea: the old Elizabethan harbour. A guidebook from 1794 wrote:

> Very large pieces of timber; the remains of the pier, are still to be seen at particular times, at low water, when the tide has swept away the beach, covered by enormous rocks, which were brought there to form the foundation; and three or four rows of piles are visible each day at half ebb which show the direction in which the pier ran.

Hastings today is no longer a port and its fishing vessels have to be registered at Rye (bearing the letters 'RX'). Every now and then there are plans submitted to construct a harbour once again in Hastings' old town, the most recent being in 2017.

The Lookout, Tackleway

Take one of many of the passageways leading off All Saints' Street and climb up to the East Hill area. Here you will find the lookout point on the edge of the cliffs, which gives breathtaking views of the town and the sea. From here you can see directly down into the area known as The Stade (a Norman word meaning 'landing place'). On a clear day you can see all the way to Eastbourne and Beachy Head along the coast.

The lookout point has been used for hundreds of years by ladies of the fishing families. Many would come to this point in the early hours of the morning to watch and wait for their loved ones coming home with a catch of fish to sell. More often than not whole families were involved in the fishing trade, with fathers, brothers and sons taking to seas that were often treacherous and deadly, many never returning to their homes.

DID YOU KNOW?
Tackleway gets its name from the old French word '*tegill*', meaning 'tile', and is not connected with fishing as many think.

The fishing beach is the heart of the old fishing quarter, offering an insight into ancient tradition and the modern way of fishing today. It's a great place to explore with hidden secrets for those who enquire. There have been net huts on this beach for centuries and you cannot mistake the tall black sheds for anything else. However, not many know that

Secrets of these tall black buildings are revealed the closer you get to them.

these were created by Spanish fishermen when they found themselves on the shores of Hastings during stormy weather. They were taken in by local folk and, as a thank you, the Spanish created the net huts so that the fishermen would always have somewhere safe and dry to store their nets and equipment. These constructions have also been known as net shops and deezes, and bear some close relationship to the clinker-built fishing boats – they are painted with black tar to keep them weatherproofed and guard against the elements on this open part of the coast. They have become a local landmark, have featured as Hastings Council's logo, and are also a favourite with artists and photographers alike.

The working fishing beach.

The lookout point was used by fishermen's wives for hundreds of years.

Winkle Club

In a central location in the old town you will find a very large winkle on Winkle Island, set proudly for all to see. This winkle relates to the Winkle Club of Hastings, which was formed many moons ago by local fishermen. Today the members are not just limited to the fishermen but also to leading citizens of the town and a few famous people too, including the Duke of Windsor and Sir Winston Churchill. Every member carries a winkle shell with them, which they must produce should they be asked to 'Winkle Up', or face a fine. Sir Winston Churchill was made a member in 1955 and presented with a solid gold winkle. The first man to challenge him was fellow winkler Lord Montgomery.

One of the streets that seldom gets fully explored is All Saints' Street. Along this quaint street you will find a modern residential passageway named Swaines Passage, named after Joseph Swaine. He was a local fisherman who was shot in 1821 by the Coast Blockade Servicemen during a smuggling affray when he was mistaken for a smuggler. He is buried in All Saints' graveyard. There was much unrest from locals following Joseph's premature death, who were deeply shocked at the death of an innocent victim.

Along this street you will find houses from many historical periods, including many fishermen's cottages. This was once known as Fish or Fisher Street due to the occupation of residents of the area.

Winkle Island.

The magnificent sculpture of the winkle on Winkle Island.

The Lord Nelson pub, the Bourne. Joseph Swaine lived in a tiny cottage at the rear of the building and was tragically killed by the customs guards.

Above: Tall and mysterious net huts on Hastings Beach.

Left: A twitten running from Tackleway down on to Rock-a-Nore and the fishing beach area.

2. Smuggling Secrets and Tales

Smugglers' Cottage, High Street

Every coastal town and village around England has historical connections to smugglers. Coves and estuaries were used by smugglers to hide their contraband goods and residents of ancient places were often roped into helping their illicit activities by concealing goods, and sometimes even the perpetrator themselves. It is believed that 90 per cent of the old town's population were involved in smuggling in some way or another in the eighteenth century, and there are many tales of the smugglers' exploits. One reminder of this time is the Smugglers' Cottage at the top of the High Street. Believed to have the largest chimney in the town, smugglers would hide some of their illicit goods in this rather obvious hiding place to fool the customs guards, who would look there and think they had found the contraband when it was in fact only a fraction of the goods hidden throughout the old town.

Rye, a close neighbour to Hastings, also has many smuggling secrets.

The Smugglers' Cottage, showing the huge chimney where contraband was hidden in secret.

DID YOU KNOW?
Owlers is a name given to the lookout men who would indicate to smugglers by sounding a hoot like an owl if the customs guards were about.

There is an elaborate maze of tiny passageways and tunnels under the street of the old town, linking East Hill and West Hill along with many of the churches, inns and houses in the old quarter. These were all used by smugglers who brought their goods ashore on the beaches and entered one of the many well-concealed tunnels, making their way to one of the many inns and their waiting customers. Once inside the tunnels, they could easily lose anyone who tried to follow them. The passages were dug out by the smugglers and the routes were handed down from generation to generation. Many customs guards were lost down the dark tunnels as anyone unfamiliar with the passages found it almost impossible to find their way out. A lot of the buildings in the old town are built on high pavements because many of the properties have interconnecting cellars. It was very common for inhabitants of a house to be interrupted by a smuggler emerging from their cellar to make his way out into the street and continue on his way.

The Smugglers' Cottage has a tiny window in its side wall facing down the High Street. Smugglers out at sea with a boat full of gold, brandy or tea needed a reliable way of knowing if and when it was safe to come ashore with their goods so they could avoid the patrolling customs guards. They would pay the residents of Smugglers' Cottage to help them by placing a lantern in the tiny window it if was safe to some ashore. The smugglers would look in the direction of the cottage as they approached the coast and if there was only darkness, they would stay out at sea until the light appeared.

The Stag Inn, All Saints' Street, has many connections with the Hastings smugglers.

One of these many passageways and tunnels can be found under the Stag Inn of All Saints' Street. This ancient inn dates back to the sixteenth century. The tunnel was discovered by a previous landlord in the 1950s when he was having some maintenance work carried out in his cellars. If you were to follow this tunnel it would lead you down through the sandstone cliffs to the beach on Rock-a-Nore. Gold coins and kegs of brandy dating from the height of the smuggling period were discovered in the tunnels, left by the smugglers in their haste to avoid capture and certain death at the hands of the customs officers.

DID YOU KNOW?
There was more tea and lace hidden up the chimney of the Smugglers' Cottage than anywhere else in the old town.

Twittens

There are passageways and twittens running all over the old town. The main thoroughfares – the High Street, George Street, the Bourne, All Saints' Street and Tackleway – are linked by a maze of interweaving passages. Their function has always been the same: to provide shortcuts for residents. Wandering along the narrow passageways, it is easy to see how the alleys provided the smugglers of Hastings with an ideal place to work. Some twittens appear to be dead ends, others double back, and some lead you to magnificent hidey-holes that you would otherwise never have found. These alleyways were also frequented by petty thieves and were not a place to linger after dark. Many locals lost their way in the passageways at night and were robbed of their jewellery, watches and money. The thieves were rarely caught because the twittens were so dark – there was some places where even the moonlight could not penetrate – that the miscreants could not be identified by their victims.

DID YOU KNOW?
Smugglers had their own nicknames, including Yorkshire George, Bulverhythe Tom and Flushing Jack.

Today these passageways still have a very creepy atmosphere if you dare to wander down them after dark. Although, thankfully, we now have modern street lighting, there are still some dark and eerie corners that the light never reaches and you can never be sure whether someone, or something, is lurking there. Many say that the passageways are home to the spirits of thieves, still lying in wait for their next victim.

A twitten – the old quarter is littered with these secret passageways.

Above left: Once the haunt of smugglers, today haunted by the past.

Above right: A twitten that locals used to cut through the town.

Right: 'Twitten' is an ancient name given to these passageways, some of which are dead ends.

Garden Cottages. This passage, or snickleway, perfectly shows the tiny alleys between houses and other buildings that litter the old town.

The Bull Inn, Bexhill Road, St Leonards

At the westernmost tip of West St Leonards is the ancient settlement of Bulverhythe, which has a fascinating and almost forgotten history. It dates back to Roman times, when the port of Bulverhythe existed mainly to transport iron ore from the quarry at Beauport. The name Bulverhythe means 'landing place for the people' and at one point it had its own little pier. During the thirteenth century Bulverhythe was a self-contained village, mainly in the area of the Galley Hill, or Gallows Head as it was known then. In the seventeenth century, Bulverhythe was the haunt of notorious smugglers and one of their favourite places to hide goods and transact illicit business was the Bull Inn.

Ale has been served on the site of the Bull since at least the thirteenth century. Entering the Bull today feels like stepping back in time; it has a magical atmosphere. The ruins of the old abbey and church can be found in the inn's back garden, stones from which are said to have been used in the construction of the old inn. Many of the beams in the building came from ships wrecked off the coast. The bar area in the Bull was once used as a courtroom and many were sentenced to death here. There were cells underneath the bar area where condemned prisoners were kept before being taken across to Galley Hill and hanged at the gallows. Deep in the cellars are two passageways leading into secret tunnels. One tunnel leads south into the cliffs at Bulverhythe; it is said to have been used by the smugglers, allowing them to enter the inn undetected. The second tunnel leads north and was used by the monks, as it linked the inn and the abbey.

The Bull Inn has connections with a famous shipwreck found off the coast here. In 1749 the *Amsterdam* ran aground at Bulverhythe Sands and sank. The vessel, one of the biggest ships of the time, had been en route to the East Indies and her nine-month voyage was to take her through the English Channel to the Scilly Isles, then out across the Atlantic Ocean to Batavia, Java. She was part of a fleet of five ships heading for Java carrying a total of 4.8 million guilders, securely stowed away in the captain's cabin. There were some 335 people on board the ship including seamen, officers, soldiers and five passengers.

She set sail on 8 January 1749 but ran into trouble less than three weeks later when she was hit by severe storms. On 26 January 1749 she sank off the coast at Bulverhythe. Conditions on board were cramped and unsanitary, and diseases such as malaria, dysentery and leprosy were rife. Many died during the first two weeks of the voyage and their bodies were removed from the wreck and buried in a small cemetery next to the Bull Inn. Those who were sick were taken to a farm in the Filsham Valley. The Bull was used as a base by the investigators from the shipping company.

The Amsterdam sank 14 feet into the sands in just one month and the wreck lay undisturbed until the 1960s, when it was eventually rediscovered – many explorations had been made previously to try and find it but they had proved unsuccessful. In 1969 civil engineers were working on an old sewer at Bulverhythe that badly needed replacing. During the course of the work storms ripped into this part of the coast and divers were brought in to access the damage caused by the weather. It was during one of these dives

DID YOU KNOW?
Women were also involved in smuggling and could easily conceal tobacco, tea and lace in their skirts.

that the remarkable discovery of the *Amsterdam* was made and items such as bottles of wine, kitchen implements and candlesticks were among the items found. A cannon was also among the items uncovered, but the lifting machinery could not hold it and it was dropped into the sands. Unfortunately, no record was kept of the items removed from the ship. Work continues on the wreck to learn more about its final journey and the lives of the people on board.

The Bull Inn, St Leonards.

Joseph Swaine, Resident and Fisherman of Hastings

Venture along All Saints' Street in the old quarter and you will notice a mixture of tiny cottages. Many of these were lived in by the numerous fishing families that this street was known for. These houses also stretched round into the area known as the Bourne until these were demolished to make way for modern improvements to the town. The fishermen were very poor and many lived with a number of family members in cramped conditions. Sons in these families were expected to follow their fathers into fishing, as this was the tradition. The Swaines were one such family and Joseph Swaine, who lived in a tiny cottage at the bottom of All Saints' Street with his family, was well known and liked in the community. In 1812 Joseph was killed by a customs guard and his death was a terrible loss to the fishing community.

Fishing provided a cover for smugglers coming into the harbour; many poor fishermen were asked to bring in goods in their fishing boats and were offered money to do so. Smugglers often disguised their boats as fishing vessels and dressed as fishermen to fool the customs guards. This worked quite well, until the customs guards realised that they were being made fools of and brought in a new rule: anyone caught impersonating a fisherman and smuggling goods would be instantly shot. This still did not deter all of the smugglers, who were crafty and clever in their operations, as the thought of the money they would get for their illicit goods was too tempting. On the night that Joseph Swaine was killed, he had been out to sea off the beach in the old town. As he returned to the shore, the customs guards assumed he was a smuggler and shot him dead. Not long after this tragic event the guards were stripped of the authority to shoot suspected smugglers, as the government realised that the Hastings fishermen were far too valuable to risk losing any more at the hand of customs officials. Joseph lives on in the memory of many local people today, and he has even had a passageway in All Saints' Street that leads up to Tackleway named after him.

There were huge amounts of money to be made from the smuggling runs. A report from the Hastings Custom House in the late winter of 1805 listed the items from one seizure:

477 Casks of Brandy	1650 gallons
109 Casks of Rum	375
421 Casks of Gin	1460
8 packages of tea	188 pounds
173 packages of tobacco	6432 pounds
2 bags of salt	97 pounds
1 Lugger and tackle	
1 Small boat	

All this has a total value of £2,784 5s 8d. It is obvious to see why so many of the Hastings population were involved in smuggling in one way or another.

DID YOU KNOW?
Waterloo Passage is said to be the most haunted passage (twitten) in the old town.

3. The Seaside Resort

Hastings and the neighbouring St Leonards and Bexhill-on-Sea have long had a grand history of being prominent seaside resorts, ever since designs were first created for such an idea along this stretch of the coastline between Eastbourne and Brighton to the west and Folkestone and Dover to the east. Today, Hastings still retains much of the traditional seaside appeal and thousands of visitors flock to the area each year.

These towns have huge seaside appeal and have done since the early eighteenth century when masses visited to take in the appeal of the sea air – this was very popular for the upper classes of society. The popularity of the seaside towns grew with the coming of the railways in 1840s, which made smaller towns more accessible to the many. The railways were completed in 1860–70 and from that point on working-class people were able to afford to travel too, which opened up a whole new world for them and saw the true birth of the British seaside resort. By the Edwardian period this tradition had grown significantly, with masses of people venturing from all over the country and taking in the delights of the sea air and the costal lifestyle.

What did people enjoy so much about a visit to the seaside? Well, first of all there was the experience of the water itself: a dip in the sea or a walk along the coast was a refreshing change to the dull town and city life many suffered day in, day out. It offered people an escape from poor working conditions and often overcrowded homes.

The first bathing machines – huts on wheels – were recorded from around the 1730s. They worked with horses pulling the hut down to the water's edge so that the female bathers would be protected at all times. They became part of Victorian society and were found at all resorts around the country. By the Edwardian period their popularity had started to die down slightly and a more liberal approach was taken to this activity. It was in Bexhill-on-Sea in 1901 that bathers of both sexes were allowed to mix on the same beach.

From around the early 1900s the interest and enthusiasm for seaside holidays and day trips took hold and developed around the country. Successful businesses were fuelled by this new activity in the form of hotels and guest houses, restaurants, cafés, theatres, cinemas, shops and no end of other facilities to accommodate these vast numbers of visitors.

East and West Hill Railways

Hastings' old town nestles delightfully between East Hill and West Hill, shaping the town into the valley that it has become known for. On the West Hill you will find Hastings Castle and St Clements Caves, and on the East Hill there are the vast open spaces of the Fairlight Country Park offering excellent walks and wildlife spotting opportunities stretching for miles along the coast. Both hills can be easily accessed on foot, but those wanting a more leisurely approach and the opportunity to take

White Rock, Hastings, showing the resort town as it was in 1927.

Hastings Pier, 2009.

in some of the breathtaking views can take one of the clifftop railways. The East Hill Cliff Railway along Rock-a-Nore Road is reportedly the second steepest in the country. It was created in 1902 and is said to have been built by hand. The West Hill Cliff Railway dates from 1891 and runs partly through a cave. It is reported that they were created in an effort to help contemporary ladies who enjoyed visiting the town but did not wish to exhaust themselves in their long skirts climbing up the many steps, which offer an alternative route to the top of the hills.

The Royal Victoria Hotel on the seafront was completed in 1828 and offered luxurious accommodation for visitors to the town and still exists today. At the back of the hotel there was once a covered walkway so that guests could cross the road without the fear of having to face the elements. To the rear of the hotel you can find the Masonic Hall, which was once used as a banqueting hall. Food and drinks were prepared at the hotel and brought to the hall via an underground tunnel. The Masonic Hall was well known for its social events and was very much a place to be seen.

Today you will find all the modern attractions of a seaside town: the pier, the brightly coloured amusement arcades, the ice cream and, of course, the fish and chips. There are also traditional hotels and guest accommodation available for those wishing to stay a little longer.

Left: The West Hill lift railway goes from George Street up to the castle and the caves. *Right*: St Mary in the Castle had everything that the Victorian visitor to Hastings needed: somewhere to stay, somewhere for entertainment, somewhere to eat and somewhere to worship.

Hastings Pier has long been one of the town's major tourist attractions. When it was first designed it was modelled on Brighton's West Pier. The building project started in 1869 and took three years to complete, costing over £20,000 at the time. It has a large pavilion at one end, which was sadly destroyed by fire in 1917. There were several small businesses dotted along the length of the pier including cafés and shops, and a shooting gallery was added in 1910 followed by a bowling alley. The pier has had an eventful history, including it being known in the 1930s as one of *the* entertainment venues on the south coast. In more recent times, in 2010 Hastings Pier was devastated by a fire that destroyed most of the pier. It has taken years of dedication and fundraising to create the modern pier you see today. Many people forget that St Leonards also had its own pier – one to rival the main Hastings one. Sadly it no longer exists today, however a plaque marks its former location along the Marina part of the promenade.

St Mary in the Castle, Hastings Seafront
This crescent is an architectural delight, but how many people stop on the opposite side of the road, look across and marvel at its design and beauty? It can only really be appreciated when you are some distance away from the building, but it is well worth the effort. During the 1780s the resident population of Hastings escalated and the numbers of visitors to the town also increased. Thomas Pelham seized the opportunity to build on his land at the foot of the cliffs and create elegant houses for the expanding local population. He decided to build a church at the centre of his creation so that residents would have somewhere

Hastings Pier today.

to worship. Huge amounts of cliff were removed and building work began in 1824. Once complete the complex would provide both leisure facilities and accommodation for residents and visitors alike, all built in a very attractive crescent overlooking the sea. Incorporated was the Marine Palace of Varieties, which opened in 1897 as the town's first music hall. It survived until 1910 when it became the Royal Cinema de Luxe. It was thought that if you provided guests with somewhere to sleep, eat, drink and be entertained then they would seldom want to venture elsewhere, therefore becoming a captive market.

St Mary in the Castle was designed in 1828 by Joseph Kay. It gets its name from the original church built in the grounds of Hastings Castle. Sadly, very little of this remains today, with only ruins visible, but it is remembered in the name of the beautiful building below it.

When St Marys was originally built it was in a Grecian style, with grand pillars and a curved design. You can see examples of this with the auditorium's curved doors and layout. Rich shades of turquoise were used in the colour palate, making it feel like the Mediterranean; at the time of construction these colours were considered to exude wealth. In the large domed ceiling you will notice an inscription in Hebrew, which roughly translates as 'The Lord Will Provide'. The complex is also home to a natural spring, which was used to supply water to an immersion font built in the twentieth century.

The auditorium itself is magnificent and you can spend time here just gazing at many wonderful things – the Victorian floor tiles, woodblock flooring, memorial tablets set into the walls, ornate plasterwork on the ceiling and the roof area, wooden pews and so much more. The sound in this auditorium is like no other building in the town and is perfect for live performances and shows.

Venture beyond the auditorium and you will come across some amazing finds, some of which leave a chill to the soul. As well as being a popular place to worship, St Marys was also a fashionable place to be buried. Deep in the crypt area you will find the catacombs, where hundreds of people were laid to rest. When extensive work was carried out in more recent times, many of the remains were moved to Wallingers Walk in the West Hill area, though some do still remain here in the catacombs.

Many of the dead were not local but from far away towns and cities, who chose to spend their last days of their lives here in Hastings and then be buried in this grand place. Funerals were conducted in the place of worship and then coffins were lowered into the crypt by a lift especially designed for the task.

Remains of this lift still exist today and can be found behind a locked door in the crypt area. Little of the actual mechanism remains, but we have been told that late at night when the building is being locked up a strange noise can be heard from behind the locked door. It's as if the old machine is trying to spring back to life. There are no reports, however, of anyone being brave enough to open the door to see what is behind!

St Leonards Pier

In 1891, the grand opening of the St Leonards Pier took place. It was situated almost opposite the Royal Victoria Hotel – an ideal position for visitors and people staying here – and became a direct rival to Hastings Pier. There was a magnificent room at the end of St Leonards Pier that was used for dancing, and a local orchestra used to play. During the Second World War, the pier was greatly reduced in size to guard against invasion and,

The plaque showing the former location of the St Leonards Pier.

Parade and Pier, St. Leonards

The Parade and St Leonards Pier.

sadly, what was left of the structure was removed in 1951. Unfortunately little remains today to tell the story of St Leonards Pier, other than a memorial stone to mark the spot.

No. 13 Croft Road, Hastings

If you walk up past St Clements Church you will turn a corner into Croft Road where you will find a mix of timber cottages and Regency houses. No. 13 Croft Road, or Lavender Cottage as it is now known, is a tiny black and white house on the left-hand side of the road. The cottage was built in the late fifteenth century and many of the beams used in its construction came from shipwrecks on the old town's beach. It is recorded that this house was one of the first small cottages to have paying guests who came to the area especially for the health-giving properties of the sea air. Over the years residents of the cottage have unearthed wooden objects while they have been carrying out work to the house; one such object is that of a wooden oar.

St Clements Caves

Just a short walk from Croft Road in an upwardly direction and you will start to climb West Hill. It is here that you will find Smugglers Adventure, also known as St Clements Caves.

BALLROOM, St. CLEMENTS CAVES, HASTINGS.

ST. CLEMENTS CAVES, HASTINGS. 16.C

Above: The Ballroom area of
St Clements Caves.

Left: A carving found deep in
St Clements Caves.

These caves are made from sandstone and it is said they were formed by locals getting sandstone from the area. However, they attracted the attention of the smugglers and so were blocked up in 1811. Some nine years later a local greengrocer by the name of Joseph Golding broke into them quite accidentally when getting sand for building purposes. It was decided to obtain permission to open them for visitors to the town. Golding obtained a formal lease and created a sculpture that allegedly represented Napoleon, and he also dug out galleries. The first illuminated exhibition took place in the caves in July 1827 when the charge was 1s 6d, which included a visit to the area of the caves known as the ballroom. The earliest illustration of the caves dates from 1786 in the *Gentleman's Magazine*. The caves have proved popular ever since and are visited by thousands each year. There are also caves on the East Hill, which were inhabited by the Butler family in the 1840s.

An Unusual Attraction

Among the better-known attractions in Hastings – chiefly the castle and the caves – was another. A young lady who visited in the winter of 1835–36 wrote of it in her journal: 'The industrious fleas, which were spending a week or so here to show off their tricks.' This was part of an exhibition of the hydro-oxygen microscope, by which a piece of French cambric was magnified to look like that of a latticed window.

It is interesting to note how the popularity of the town really grew throughout the nineteenth century as an article in the *Illustrated Times* in 1857 gives an account of what visitors to the town did, which sounds quite different to that of today:

> We have visitors here of all sorts from the noble lord to the poor London warehouseman, who comes down with his family by the excursion train on Sunday to get nine hours by the seaside. On Sunday, shoals of Londoners swarm upon the beach, wandering listlessly about with apparently no other aim than to get a mouthful of fresh air.

St Leonards the Resort

The architectural design of St Leonards was centred around a Hydro, Assembly Rooms and a subscription private garden. Today the Hydro is the Royal Victoria Hotel, the Assembly Rooms are the Masonic Hall and the private gardens are St Leonards Gardens. All still retain their original grandness.

A walk through St Leonards Gardens is a real treat and you will no doubt reach the archway in Maze Hill. This is now private residences and one of the houses – North Lodge – was once home to the famous novelist Sir Henry Rider Haggard, who lived here for many years. A long-forgotten tollgate was once established here also, although today you can travel through the archway for free.

East Hill Arches

There are some rather mysterious arches that can be found on the side of the East Hill. They appear in one of the illustrations of the first guidebook to the area in 1794, but are seldom mentioned again. They were believed to have been carved by John Coussens (1750–1836) in the late 1780s and many think that this was fuelled by a desire to create antiquities during the Georgian times when there was a distinct lack of them in the town.

4. Crime and Punishment

Like any other town, Hastings has had its fair share of criminal goings-on over the centuries. In fact, it has its own museum dedicated to the subject of crime, which offers a fascinating insight into the criminal world.

The True Crime Museum is housed in a series of caves accessed via Palace Avenue Arcade at White Rock on the Hastings seafront. The arcade and caves formed part of the Palace Court Hotel, which was built in 1885 by the architect Arthur Wells on the site of a former brewery. (You will see that Cave 1 of the museum is paved with brick at a slight inclination, which was to facilitate the rolling of beer barrels down tracks towards the bricked-over entrance by the 'Luminol' exhibit.) The caves were created by extending existing fissures in the sandstone cliff face. Miners from Cornwall who were working on local railway tunnels at the time were drafted in to do the work – their pickaxe marks are still visible on the surface of Caves 1, 3 and 4.

Built to profit from the popularity of the new nearby Hastings Pier, the lofty hotel boasted superb views, luxury accommodation, drinking and dining provided by 'chefs from London's top Piccadilly restaurants'. It was one of the first buildings on the south coast to be lit by

The True Crime Museum, White Rock.

Palace Court above the True
Crime Museum.

electricity. The huge loud generators providing this power were hidden away in the caves behind the hotel and their fixing points can still be seen in Caves 3 and 4 of the museum. These generators also powered the fabulous central lift system, which can be seen through the main entrance doors and were featured in the recent Neil Jordan vampire film *Byzantium.*

The hotel, however, proved too expensive for most early twentieth-century holidaymakers and closed in 1917. Canadian soldiers and RAF personnel were billeted in the hotel towards the end of the First World War. In 1926 Captain Vincent Moss converted it into the luxury seafront apartments called Palace Chambers. The bar and restaurant (Palace Bars) later became a meeting place for artists and bohemians, including occultist and Hastings resident Aleister Crowley. Druid ceremonies were already being conducted in the caves and it is likely that the raised platform in the museum (now containing the original acid vats used by serial killer John George Haigh) was built to hold the Druid altar. Fixing points for benches or pews can also still be seen in Cave 1.

Public Executions and Punishment

With so many alehouses and inns dotted around the old town area, it's not surprising that vast amounts of alcohol frequently led to unacceptable behaviour by the townsfolk. There was one report from March 1826 that a man was found to be lying in Courthouse Street in a very drunk state; he was later fined 5s. On another occasion a man by the name of

John Daniel was found intoxicated around the streets of the Bourne and threw his wife out of his house for three or four hours. When he was approached he was described as being very abusive. In another instance it was reported that two ladies were found lying incapable in the street and placed in a watch house overnight for their own safety.

DID YOU KNOW?
In 1848 Courthouse Street was known as Union Street.

On 9 May 1836 the town saw a major change: the introduction of the Hastings Police Force. It comprised of one inspector, three superintendents or sergeants and nine constables. Applicants had to be between the ages of twenty-one and forty, at least 5-foot 7-inches tall and also had to be able to read and write fully. They obtained sixty applications from men to join the force from this recruitment drive, from all ages and backgrounds. By the end of the first year of the force being established there had been 167 people arrested, 129 of which were convicted.

It is interesting to learn of the punishments that have been handed out in the Hastings area. Execution by drowning was the usual means of execution in a Cinque Ports town, although many offenders from other Cinque Ports were buried alive. Execution by hanging, which included the gibbeting or the hanging by chains near the scene of the crime, was another method. This was the case for a Thomas Wolfe from Southwark, who in 1611 murdered John Martyn from Hastings somewhere towards the west end of present-day George Street. Thomas was hanged on the spot of the crime and as this was on a route in and out of the town, it was hoped it would deter others.

Stocks were a common site in towns up and down the country from 1405, when it became law that every town and village be provided with a pair of them. You would usually find them close to a public space, for example on the village green. The guilty person was made to sit with their legs held by the stocks for a specified length of time. The one benefit to this was that the offender's hands were free, so they would be able to defend themselves should the need arise. This punishment was used for such crimes as drunkenness or for neglect of your work duty. The stocks were used in Hastings and their last recorded use here was in 1840, with them finally being removed in 1848. One other form of punishment used in Hastings was the ducking stool. The offender was tied onto the wooden structure then lowered into the water. This was commonly used on women who had too free a tongue and were unable to be curtailed by any other form of punishment.

Around Hastings you will find buildings and locations that have connections with law and order; many are well hidden while others are more obvious. Courthouse Street has numerous buildings connected with law and order as it is where the original Court Hall once stood, along with the old Town Hall (which served the area until 1881 when it became the police station) and the old town museum. There is also the rather impressive Victorian Gothic Town Hall in Queens Road.

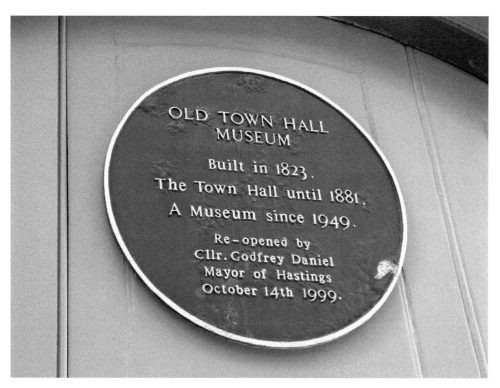

The Old Town Hall plaque on the High Street.

Site of the old gaol on Courthouse Street.

Courthouse Street, the old site of execution.

There have been four town halls on three different sites in Hastings over the years. After the Second World War the old Town Hall was used as a branch of the public library and the Museum of Local History.

Courthouse Street today lies between the main Bourne Road and the High Street, and has a wonderful assortment of little shops to explore. The street has led an interesting and colourful life and has seen public executions and punishments over the centuries. A medieval courthouse once stood here, but this was sadly demolished in 1820 to make way for the town goal. The Kings Head Inn once stood on the corner of Courthouse Street, where it meets the Bourne, and was a popular place on execution day as it was an ideal spot to view them from.

At one time every town was issued with a pair of stocks by law. Between 1832 and 1840 the stocks in the old town were used solely for offences to do with drunkenness. The stocks and pillory, which were only used for petty crimes, were forms of entertainment to the locals, who would jeer and throw objects such as rotten fruit and dead animals and fish at the poor unfortunate souls.

DID YOU KNOW
At the top of Old London Road there was once a gibbet, located as a warning to new visitors to the town to behave during their stay.

The ancient town of Winchelsea lies a few miles east of Hastings on the A259 towards Rye. Wandering around the quaint streets of the town, you really do get a feel for the past as you explore the little shops and inns and the wonderful churchyard. The town played its own colourful part in the smuggling history of the area, and also took a battering from the French when they invaded during the fourteenth and fifteenth centuries. Opposite St Thomas' Church lies a wonderful ancient building, which is said to be the oldest building in the town. It is known as the Great Hall and it holds a secret. Part of this historical building used to serve as the town goal, holding many smugglers and other wrongdoers in its time. There were often reports of overcrowding and poor conditions here.

Ninfield is a small village on the edge of Bexhill, a quiet unassuming place in a semi-rural location. It is here, in what seems to be an idyllic setting, that you can find one of Sussex's best survivals: some rare iron stocks with an attached whipping post. They offer a fascinating glimpse into the past.

The central Town Hall, Queens Road.

Left: A plaque telling of the old Courthouse building.

Below: The old Courthouse building.

Aleister Crowley

One of Hastings' most notorious residents was Aleister Crowley, who spent the end of his life here.

Hastings has a long history of witchcraft and sinister goings-on. Witches tried to settle in the town in its early years but were cast out. Many criminals who were caught also claimed to be witches to try and get off with a lesser punishment, but this seldom worked. The famous occultist Alesiter Crowley spent time in the town, practising magic of various types and also partaking in criminal activities. While black witches were believed to have sacrificed animals in the castle grounds, Crowley claimed to have sacrificed humans – but nothing could be proved.

Crowley died in 1967 from a heroin overdose, believed to have been enough to have killed forty-seven elephants. He placed a curse on the people of Hastings on his deathbed. He recognised that Hastings has mysterious and secret powers and it was this that lured many people to the place, and for this he hated the town. He placed a curse that stated should a local ever want to leave for good then they must find a white pebble from the beach with a hole directly through it and carry it with them wherever they go, otherwise they would be destined to keep returning until their dying day.

Sweeney Todd

Another criminal who it is said to have spent time in Hastings was Sweeney Todd. (Sweeney is a fictional character first mentioned in the nineteenth-century penny dreadful series *The String of Pearls,* though there are claims he was based on a historical figure.) Sweeney's tale is one of hardship and sadness. It is said that due to his ill fortune and neglectful parents Sweeney travelled to Hastings in search of work, which he was lucky enough to find at a butcher's shop called Harris the Butchers in the High Street of the old town. Mr Harris was keen to take Sweeny on as an apprentice as he was very skilled with the knives. Sweeney was only fourteen years old when he started work here. It is said he was pleased to find such a position and thought himself doubly lucky because Mr Harris also had a young and beautiful daughter who Sweeney planned to marry. However, when he finally plucked up the courage to propose to Miss Harris she turned him down. He had not expected this reaction and felt a terrible desire to slit her throat so that she could not tell anyone of his proposal. So one night Sweeney crept into the upstairs room of the butcher's shop and found Miss Harris doing some paperwork; she was all alone as her father had gone out for the evening. Sweeney took his chance and with one stroke of the knife she was dead. He dragged her body downstairs, cut it up and, it is said, made her into sausages and pies to sell in the shop.

Sweeney Todd left Hastings in 1762 and returned to London, where he was caught pickpocketing and sent to Newgate Gaol until he was nineteen. After his release, he set up a barber's shop in Fleet Street and the rest is 'history'.

DID YOU KNOW?
Hastings' present-day Town Hall is said to be haunted by a cat.

5. In Sickness and in Health

Today the medical care and attention provided by the National Health Service (NHS) can sometimes be taken for granted. Some patients turn to private medicine to try and help them and others look at alternative remedies. How many of us, though, think about how far medicine has come over the years and the advancements that have been made since the times of the plague and smallpox epidemics?

During the sixteenth century, like many other places in England, infectious disease was rife. Many Hastings residents suffered from a great number of afflictions, which sadly we know little about, though they were all as feared and as dreaded as the plague as so little was known and understood about the subject.

The worst local plague epidemic was in 1563 when just under 200 people in Hastings died from the disease. Public fairs were cancelled and people were banned from visiting the town in case of bringing in the disease and spreading it. After the plague came small pox, which was prominent in Hastings in 1729 until 1731 and resulted in further deaths in the town. One idea to try and reduce the risk of infection was the establishment of pesthouses, one of which was in the old town close to the fish market. Influenza was responsible for 182 deaths in 1810.

DID YOU KNOW?
There is said to be a plague pit at Coburg Place where victims were buried.

The Old Apothecary

With many advancements in medical science occurring through the early to mid-1800s, it is of little surprise that Hastings was known for making its own discoveries and was even described as being 'hospital minded', with many of the townsfolk being generous towards related charities.

One of the town's oldest buildings is the Hastings Dispensary, which was established in the old town in 1834. It can be found at the bottom of the High Street on the raised pavement in a building that was formerly the Royal Oak Hotel.

Catherine Cookson

Catherine Cookson is best known for her writing and her books portraying life in the poorest communities of England. She is seldom remembered for her life in Hastings and her work in medicine. Catherine Cookson (née McMullen) came to Hastings in 1930 and took on the 'laundry manageress' position at the workhouse. This later became known as the Municipal Hospital.

In 1932, Catherine bought a house in Hastings called the Hurst at No. 114 Hoads Wood Road, and it was from here that she set up a house for people suffering from tuberculosis (TB), epilepsy and other such illnesses and conditions. In 1940, Catherine married Tom Cookson at St Mary Star of the Sea Church in the High Street. They continued to love at the Hurst until 1954, when they moved to a larger house in St Helens Park Road called Loreto. In her later years Catherine returned to her home area in the north-east of England and she and Tom remained there from 1976–97, when she passed away close to her ninety-second birthday.

Site of White Rock Theatre

The impressive White Rock Theatre is situated directly opposite Hastings Pier. Many famous stars have graced the stage over the years and brought in the crowds. The theatre was built in a colonial design – there are other examples of the architect's work along Bexhill Road. The theatre today is an ideal venue for residents of the town and is very popular with all ages, hosting many local festivals each year such as the Music Festival. The theatre also offers a superb bar and café where you can gaze out to sea and watch the world go by. The site, however, was once home to a slightly less glamorous building, Hastings Infirmary – the area known today as the Sussex Room was the old mortuary. The old infirmary hospital was built on this site due to the health-giving properties attributed to the sea air; however, for some patients the sight of the sea had a detrimental effect, sending them into a state of paranoid trances. It was also recorded that the rooms of the hospital had no corners so that germs and disease had nowhere to hide.

White Rock Theatre is the site of the old infirmary.

The old infirmary had round rooms so no disease could lurk in the corners.

The site of the old mineral baths, now the Source Park.

Just along from the White Rock Theatre is the area known as White Rock, where today you will find Source Park. This is the world's largest underground skate park and BMX facility, and has saved a significant part of the town's historical architecture. The White Rock Baths were once located beneath your feet here; customers would pay to immerse themselves in the health-giving properties of the mineral baths. This was hugely popular in the Victorian times and for those spending time by the sea added to their recovery from illness.

The Old Buchanan Hospital

The old Buchanan Hospital in St Leonards was the maternity hospital for the area and many locals were born here. This old hospital, with its winding corridors, closed once the maternity services were transferred to the Conquest Hospital, a purpose-built state-of-the-art hospital on the edge of the town. Some historical artefacts were rescued, including some magnificent stained-glass windows from the chapel and other areas of the hospital. These are now on display in certain areas of Conquest Hospital and certainly brighten up the place.

There are mentions of stained-glass windows as far back as the seventh century and by the fourteenth century they were considered an art form. Little has changed in their manufacture, with fragments of coloured glass being held together by an intricate lead framework. In medieval times, fables were popular and these were portrayed in many window designs. During the seventeenth and eighteenth centuries there was a decline in this craft but the nineteenth century saw an attempt to recapture the art of the window maker.

Stained-glass windows are used to depict stories from the Bible and historical events. It is believed that many of the windows hold secret messages and they have also been used to tell enchanting tales or commemorate events. The different colours used also have significant meanings. The use of black meant death; blue symbolised heavenly love and the Virgin Mary; violet meant love, truth, passion or suffering; and the use of white or gold meant innocence of the soul and holiness in life. The size of people or objects in the windows indicated their importance. Several symbols were used in the Christian church including a dove, which indicates the gentle, pure and loving influence of God. If the dove was carrying a leaf in its beak, this symbolised forgiveness. Water was used to show a basic need that all life cannot live without. It is thought that the images in the windows may have been used to educate the masses, who had little or no schooling, and to tell them the ways of the Church.

St Helens Hospital

St Helens Hospital once stood in Frederick Road. The site is now occupied by smart private residences that give no indication of what used to stand here. The hospital was a bleak place and had a very uneasy atmosphere. The original building was built as a workhouse in the 1830s and became a hospital in the 1860s. Many say that petty criminals were often sent to the workhouse and treated for insanity – most of the patients never left.

The site of the old St Helens Hospital, Frederick Road, is now a residential development.

Elizabeth Blackwell and Sophie Jex Blake

Throughout the history of Hastings there have been many discoveries and monumental occasions. One such discovery was from Dr Elizabeth Blackwell, a pioneer who fought for female advancement in the field of medicine. She lived at Rock House, Exmouth Place, Hastings, where she died in 1910 at the age of seventy-nine. She was the first woman to graduate in medicine and the first woman to be placed on the British Medical Register. She had led a remarkable life. She immigrated to America as a young girl with her family and it was there that she decided to take up the study of medicine. She found the prejudice there very difficult to deal with and was refused admission to many medical schools; however, she was finally accepted at a small school close to the Canadian border and it was from here that she graduated in 1849. She later went to France and gained some experience in nursing, where she contracted ophthalmia and lost the use of one of her eyes. She then returned to the UK and entered St Bart's Hospital in London as a graduate. She also spent some time in New York and set up a practice, but eventually settled in England, founding the National Health Society in 1871. She had returned due to ill health, and it was in Hastings that she sadly passed away. She was a remarkable lady and her achievements were amazing. So little is known about her, yet she must not be forgotten for her advancements in medicine.

One of Dr Blackwell's students was Sophia Jex Blake, who was born at Croft Place in 1840 and was christened at St Clements Church. She too had an interest and passion for learning medicine and studied and graduated in New York; however, when she returned back to England she was refused admission to many medical schools in London and Edinburgh. Eventually, after many years of battle and conflict, Sophia Jex Blake was able to set up a practice and became a successful doctor in Edinburgh. She later moved to London where she set up the London School of Medicine for Women. We owe a lot to these two remarkable ladies.

The Workhouses

In May 1753 there was much unrest in the parishes and a great gathering of parish officers was held. Up until then each parish had to bear the burden of their own poor, but they were now hoping to work together and have one workhouse for them all. This was agreed and an area of land for it was identified: the Pilchard House in George Street (now home to the antique centre and an Indian restaurant). Notes from the time do not speak kindly of the new workhouse and frequently describe the house as being full of bugs. The inmates were forced to live in poor conditions and were even accused of causing an outbreak of smallpox in the town; however, after inspection by a doctor, it was discovered that the itching among the poor was caused by the bugs.

When people entered into these houses they normally brought all their belongings with them. Should they later leave, they would need to seek permission to take the items with them. One such account is from Sarah Wood in 1764, who was allowed to bring the apparel she was wearing with several small things in an oaken chest, along with her bed, one pair of sheets, two blankets, a tea kettle, warming pan, brass kettle and an iron pot. Another family, however, were only permitted to take their clothes.

The old Union Workhouse, George Street.

The workhouses were often blamed for harbouring disease and so in 1765 a new doctor was appointed to look after the people at the workhouse: Mr Thomas Parnell, a surgeon. He agreed that, for 18 guineas a year, he would attend to and furnish all poor people that may happen to fall ill in the town. It was also agreed that all cases of smallpox would be removed to the pesthouse.

DID YOU KNOW?
The main hospital site for the town was originally where the White Rock theatre stands today.

Battle and its Place in Medical History

As is true of all places, the practice of medicine in the town of Battle took many forms over the ages, and Battle Abbey played a central role in the provision of medicine in the medieval settlement. After the dissolution, we know of at least one doctor – Edmund Langdon – in the early seventeenth century.

By the 1850s Battle was a particularly unhealthy place to live. The Cresy Report depicts a town with open sewers where cholera, typhoid and malaria are rife.

The sometimes gruesome tale of early medicine is illustrated by the leech jar, the Waterloo teeth and muscle rub that was used for both people and horses! A small bottle of this illustrates the story of a 'quack'. Dr Kendall was a respected, well-liked doctor who not only had his own general practice but also worked as the doctor at the Union Workhouse. He would treat the poor for free and was greatly admired by his patients.

Thomas Holloway founded Royal Holloway College (now part of the University of London) in 1884 from the vast profits he made from his pills – largely 'quack' medicine.

Battle Museum is home to some remarkable objects, one being human teeth that are said to date from the early nineteenth century. It is not known for sure whether the teeth in the denture were extracted from the jaws of dead soldiers on the battlefield of Waterloo, but it is certain the practice went on.

Gout treatment medication. (Photo kindly provided by Battle Museum)

Left: Medical scales. (Photo kindly provided by Battle Museum)

Below: No one can be sure how these teeth were obtained! (Photo kindly provided by Battle Museum)

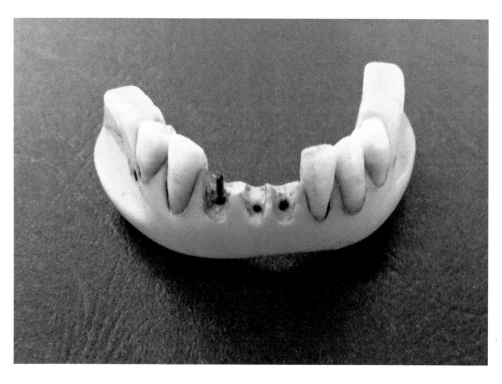

6. Life and Death

The Mortuary House, No. 135 All Saints' Street

This house is the keeper of many secrets. It dates back to the sixteenth century, when it was a merchant's house. It was constructed around the time of the Spanish Armada in 1588. The rear wing of the property – now the kitchen – is the oldest part of the house and was constructed as a complete house in its own right. The house's freestanding timber frame is said to date from the 1400s and is thought to have been dismantled from another site and erected where it now stands today. It is of a two-bay construction and is deceptive in size when viewed from the front, as it has four levels and extends back deeply from the road. There are four upper rooms that hold hidden trapdoors (coffin hatches), a front parlour and middle parlour kitchen, and a double-height rear wing that houses a kitchen and a dining room in a semi-underground cellar. There is also a backyard with an outdoor toilet and shower.

DID YOU KNOW?
In the 1700s Dr Baillie commented how excellent the climate was in Hastings for people with any sort of chest problem. This sparked the town's health tourism.

No. 135 All Saints' Street is Grade II listed and is one of the most intact and atmospheric Tudor houses in Hastings' old town. Today it is a private residence, owned and restored by Alastair Hendy (who also owns A. G. Hendy & Co., the hardware store in the High Street). It has central heating and electricity, so is perfectly habitable.

The house holds a dark secret, however. Up until the 1950s the rear wing was used as an undertaker's workshop, and cadavers were stored in the adjoining cellar room. Coffins were also made here. Two elderly Hastings fisherman have recently recounted that when they were boys they would come to the Wilderness (as this upper section of All Saints' Street was then known), peer through the back windows of the house to spot the bodies laid out, then run away.

Builders working on the house during a recent restoration occasionally heard footsteps treading the boards above in the attic rooms and crossing the coffin hatch, yet when they called up there was answer.

Many people wonder why the house appears to lean. This is because it did not originally stand at the end of a terrace, but was flanked on both sides by properties built at the same time. The Tudor house that stood on the south side crumbled into its own cellar.

Secrets are revealed inside Mortuary House. (Image kindly provided by A. Hendy)

The magic that awaits the visitor to the Mortuary House. (Image kindly provided by A. Hendy)

The Victorians built next door, leaving a twitten (a narrow footpath) in between. This left No. 135 with little support, and its exposed south wall has been on the move ever since. Note how much it tilts out towards its upper floors. This caused significant structural damage and was not addressed until its second major life-saving restoration, which began in 2006.

The house you see now is the product of two major restoration programmes in recent years. The first was in 1974–80 and was carried out by Paul Lewis; the second was in 2006–11 and by Alastair Hendy. Hendy has sympathetically restored every surface and internal fixture and reconstructed the evolution of the house as it might have happened when utilities such as plumbing and lighting first came into domestic use. This restoration has allowed it to breathe and, without trying to recreate a Tudor past, the rooms have been humbly furnished to reflect the character of the house. Hendy describes the result as 'putting back the years, the years have taken away and he has produced an environment quite unlike conventional "restored" interiors. One visitor remarked, 'It's been done-up, but not "done-up".'

The timber arrangement on the front façade is of close vertical stud construction and the south-facing wall is small-panelled and is all original. The timbers on the south-facing wall and nearest the front door bear the carpenter's marks. Originally, the front elevation would have had a gabled roof extending over a jettied first-floor window, similar to the adjacent houses; however, this was removed when the house was modernised in the eighteenth century. The Georgians despised Tudor style and ornamentation, and as such two highly carved barge boards that made up the gable were removed, but rather than being discarded they were put to practical use and still exist on the house today. If you look up where the guttering runs along the front you will see that one of these richly carved and ornamented gables is just visible, yet now reversed and acting as a wall plate to support the rafters.

DID YOU KNOW?
The Mortuary House is home to some of the last remaining original coffin hatches in the town.

The two small windows that flank the central first-floor window are original. These were covered up with wattle and daub during Georgian modernisation and so, by happenstance, much of the fine diamond leadwork and coloured glass has been preserved. These are the only original windows to survive.

The house frontage was stripped of its Georgian brickwork and render, revealing the front you see today. The front door was put back to its original position. Up until 1974, the front door was sited down a side passage on the right-hand side of the property – it opened into what is now the middle parlour kitchen, off a sort of internal twitten that then provided public access through the houses. Evidence from notches cut into the

Mortuary House, All Saints' Street.

beams showed the front door was originally situated on the left-hand side, and so this has been put back to where it is today. The twitten was blocked off and the window you now see on the right was put in its place.

Today this house is open to visitors during bank holidays and other major festivals in the town's calendar of events.

Wallingers Walk Cemetery

Venture up and over the West Hill and you will come across an area known as Wallingers Walk, where you will find a small hidden cemetery. This is a tranquil spot wildlife has made their home. It was the cemetery of St Mary-in-the-Castle and operated between 1828 and 1900. It has now been turned into a small public park. There is no chapel or other building here in the grounds and most of the gravestones have disappeared while others that have fallen over moved to the perimeter walls. All those that remain and are legible and accessible have been recorded. It is worth the climb up to the cemetery and is a lovely spot to stop and watch the world go by away from hectic modern life.

Piece of Cheese Cottage

If you venture along a twitten called Starrs Cottages, off All Saints' Street, you will be immediately met by a bright yellow triangle-shaped house known as the Piece of Cheese Cottage. This house was built in 1871 when the Starrs brothers (local builders at the time) took on the challenge to build a house on the unusual-shaped piece of land. They took on the task with open arms and created what we see today. It has had various functions over the years; artists and authors have loved its quirkiness, and at one time it was home to a little museum. What is of even further interest is that at one point the upstairs of the cottage was used as a coffin-maker's studio. Now, if you were to view the interior of this cottage, you would realise that there is no way that a coffin would be able to be lowered down the staircase. A pulley was therefore attached to the outside of the property to allow the coffins to be attached and lowered into the passageway below.

Today the house is a holiday home, enabling those who want to immerse themselves in history to spend a few nights in this unique cottage. The house does have a preservation order on it: to always stay yellow in colour and shaped like a piece of cheddar cheese.

The Piece of Cheese Cottage was built as a bet in 1871.

This was once a coffin-maker's workshop.

It has a pulley device that was used for attaching the wooden caskets.

No. 13 Croft Road

No. 13 Croft Road is also an old burial site. This was discovered a few years ago when essential work was being carried out on the pipes. The graveyard was located in the Croft Road area and extended underneath the cottages. The remains have since been moved to another location.

Graves were found during some recent excavation works on Croft Road.

Burials from St Clements have been found in the road area and underneath the houses of Croft Road.

The Old Post Office, High Street

Halfway up the High Street is the old post office, a building that held a dark secret for many years. The post office was once the heart of the community and people used it as a meeting point. However, all that now remains to remind us of the building's previous function is the red Royal Mail collection box set into the outside wall. The building, which had lain empty for decades, was saved from ruin in the 1960s and extensive reconstruction work was carried out on the interior rooms. However, workmen found more than just spiders hiding in the upstairs rooms, they uncovered a secret that had been locked away and was never expected to be found.

In the mid-nineteenth century the shop was owned by the Farrow family. The two sons, Samuel and Timothy, ran the family coffin-making business. They were skilled in the craft of coffin making and took great care over each piece that they created. The Farrows were well known and respected in the old town community. However, Samuel and Timothy's mutual hatred was also well known in the area. Even as young children they never got on and as they got older their intense dislike continued to grow. When they became responsible for the family business, though, they had to find a way of working together.

One day the brothers were seen fighting in the High Street outside their business. Onlookers feared for Samuel's life because Timothy was giving him a severe beating. They witnessed Samuel being knocked to the ground and then being dragged up the staircase, to the side of the shopfront, and into the upstairs rooms. No one ever knew what caused the argument, but was it was the worst fight that anyone had ever seen. Little did they know that they would never witness another fight between the two brothers again.

DID YOU KNOW?
Locals had to get their water from the Bourne stream, which was not always clean by the time it reached the old town as some people upstream were using it as a drain.

Local residents became worried about Samuel when he was no longer seen around the community, and when they enquired about his whereabouts they were told he had decided he could not work with Timothy anymore so had moved away to family in the country. No one thought any more about it. The years went by and Timothy eventually died at the old age of ninety-four. It is said that he carried on making coffins until his dying day – when his body was found he had been working on his own coffin.

The building stood empty for years after Timothy's death. No one ventured near the place as it had an eerie atmosphere surrounding it. It was badly neglected until the 1960s, when work began to turn it back into the attractive building it had once been. No one had been inside since the day Timothy was carried out in his coffin and there was a great deal of work to do in clearing old wood and materials from the upstairs rooms. There were also many coffins standing in one corner of the workshop, which were lifted and carried down the stairs.

When one of the builders lifted up a coffin he felt something move inside. Intrigued, he removed the coffin lid – which has been nailed down, although none of the others had sealed lids. Inside was a skeleton in a hunched-up position with the hands pressed against the inside of the coffin lid. The builders felt a cold chill, wondering just what they had discovered.

The skeleton was sent away for examination and work was carried out on the remains to try and establish who it could be. The results shocked many, but also solved a long-standing mystery. It was discovered that the skeleton found sealed in a coffin was that of Samuel Farrow, who had disappeared so many years ago. It is thought that Samuel was dragged upstairs after he had been knocked unconscious by his brother during the fight in the High Street. Thinking Samuel was dead Timothy sealed him in a coffin, but he was actually still alive. Researchers found marks on the inside of the coffin lid that had been made by Samuel's nails as he tried to claw his way out of the coffin in which he had been entombed.

7. Getting About – Transport

For centuries the only way to travel to Hastings was by sea, as the roads were extremely bad (little seems to have changed on that regard). However the town was soon to realise that if it did not take action to improve its transport links it would lose out to competition along the coast – Brighton to the west and Dover and Folkestone to the east.

Coaching Inns

There used to be a number of coaching inns around Hastings; one of the last remaining examples is No. 23 High Street. It is a private residence today, surrounded by small shops and houses, but at one time the area behind this grand house was a coaching station. A thrice-weekly stagecoach from Hastings to London was introduced in 1794. The coach left at 5 a.m. and arrived in Tunbridge Wells by 12 p.m., before continuing on its journey to London. Several coaching stations cropped up around the old town, as well as coaching inns. The coaching station at the rear of No. 23 would have been a very busy, bustling area with people and packages destined for important towns and ports. Today all that remains of this building's secret past are some original cobbles with grooves cut into them to help the horses from slipping on the stones.

The speed of the coaches was dependent on the state of the roads. To help with these costs several toll gates were introduced. In theory the money gained from the tolls should have been enough to keep the roads in question in good repair, but sadly little was done and so the Turnpike Trust – which was set up to address these issues – was often in debt.

The year 1835 saw the introduction of a new coach, *The Royal Victoria*, which went from the Victoria Hotel, St Leonards, and saw the run to London take under seven hours – the Hastings coaches took more than nine. The 1840s saw coaches heading to destinations other than London, such as Eastbourne and Lewes.

The Coming of the Railways

During the 1840s many projects were set up around the implementation of the railways; however, it was not until 1842 that the South Eastern line from London to Staplehurst was opened with a coach linking to Hastings. In 1841 the London to Brighton railway was opened and extended to include Lewes and Hastings, making these towns more accessible to the many.

Trade was to greatly benefit from the railways. In fact, the development of railways to Hastings started a new chapter in the life of the town. Sadly, however, this brought about the demise of the coaches, which could not complete with the speed of the railways. The last of the coaches ran in 1847.

DID YOU KNOW?
The Railway Hotel opened in 1851 for those who travelled to the town by train.

Above: The coming of the railways made Hastings more accessible to many visitors. Here is the railway bridge at the top of Queens Road.

Below: The modern Hastings railway station.

Sidney Little, Underground Car Park, Hastings Seafront

Sidney Little was born in Carlisle in 1885 and is best known as being a civil engineer. He worked in Ipswich for a while and then moved to Hastings, where he became the borough water engineer in 1926. During his twenty-four years working in this role he was

Postcards showing the trams in Hastings town centre.

Postcard from 1926 depicting the tram network in Hastings.

responsible for implementing many major projects throughout the town, many of which we pass by every day and give little thought to.

He is known along the south coast of England as the Concrete King, as he was a mastermind when it came to using this material for projects in the town. He installed improvements to the sea defences, allowing for the creation of the first underground car parks in the UK. The creation of these car parks meant that visitors could park their cars directly on the seafront in safe and well-lit car parks. His creation was also out of sight and so did not spoil the appearance of the area.

He also created what is known as Bottle Alley, which is a long and covered promenade with concrete panels consisting of thousands of particles of glass inserted for decoration. He was also involved in many other major projects around the town.

Unfortunately, his advancements in concrete brought with it some enemies, due to his eagerness to clear areas of historic buildings in return for the creation of road schemes.

8. Leisure Time, Activities and Sporting Pursuits

For residents and visitors alike, today's Hastings contains many opportunities for hobbies, activities and sport for leisure, from numerous sports such as rowing, football and tennis, or walking and rambling in parks, gardens and the surrounding countryside, to visiting museums and galleries. However, the way in which we carry out our hobbies and interests may have slightly changed over the centuries, and places that were once well known and loved may no longer exist, gone to make way for more modern living. Let's uncover some secrets of leisure in Hastings.

Cricket

Hastings was once famous for its cricket pitch and had regular matches in a unique town centre location. Sadly little remains today to remind us of its sporting past, only the statue dedicated to the game located in the Priory Meadow Shopping Centre. There are records of the importance of the sport to the town as early as 1745, when John Collier wrote to his father of plans he had made to attend and watch a 'great match at Cricket between Kent and all England', saying he would tell him all about it when they next met.

One of the first recorded local cricket matches was played on East Hill in 1822 between gentlemen from Bexhill and Hastings. The first Hastings Cricket Club was formed in 1840 and played on a field on the West Hill, which is now covered by the Collier Road area. There were strong links between the mayoral office and the cricket matches as each year the mayor was seen on the Central Cricket Ground enjoying a day or more at the County Cricket. The Central Cricket Ground was located so that both the mayor's parlour and the town clerk's office at the Town Hall in Queens Road could overlook the games when it was opened in 1865 – known then as the Central Cricket and Recreation Ground.

Many games of note were played here. In 1875, W. G. Grace scored 210 for the South of England against Hastings and District. There was also an annual Hastings Cricket Week, which was started in 1887 and created a great interest in first-class cricket – it later changed its name to the Hastings Festival. In 1982, Hastings Council voted to relocate the Central Cricket Ground to Summerfields in another part of the town and use the redevelop the former site as a shopping centre. It took until 1986 for all parties to agree on this move. The ground was demolished and replaced with the Priory Meadow Shopping Centre, which opened in 1997. A 10-foot sculpture by Allan Sly, *The Spirit of Cricket*, is the only reminder of the area's significant past.

The cricket ball sculpture in the shopping centre stands on the site of the old cricket ground.

Walking and Rambling

Many local young Victorian women enjoyed walking over to Fairlight Glen and Lovers' Seat. The Countess of Waldergrave, who owned the land, had strictly forbidden the sale or consumption of any alcohol (or other such items) anywhere nearby. As many ladies and young women enjoyed the area, and strolled its heights quite frequently without an escort, it was felt that it would not do for them to have to put up with the rudeness and insolence of late wassaillers on the lonely paths and dense woodland.

The Countess of Waldergrave greatly appreciated the view from here, which many others shared: 'Look upward at the glorious sky, downwards at the not less glorious sea, dotted with ships of all rig and from all nations, and sideways into the lovely dream like glen, and say can the heart want in the way of the picturesque more than this.'

Lovers' Seat, Fairlight, near Hastings.

John Logie Baird

There are many aspects of modern life that we all take for granted today: transport, medical care and items around the home. But how often do we consider their humble beginnings or their impact on the world?

In the heart of Hastings town centre you will find Queens Road, running from the memorial up to the gates of Alexandra Park. Many grand properties were constructed along this route, showing some of the best of grand Victorian architecture. If you walk along this stretch of the town centre look up to see ornate plaster designs here and there, among other architectural features.

Off the lower part of Queens Road, just round the corner from the cinema building, you will find Queens Avenue and an arcade joining York Buildings. This arcade was built around the same time as the Town Hall, when Victorian Hastings was moving out of the confines of the old town and to the west. The main part of the arcade is constructed from an ornamental iron and glass roof, offering the visitor protection from the elements.

John Logie Baird moved to Hastings in 1922 – it is thought for health reasons – after spending time in London. He first lived with a friend at No. 21 Linton Crescent. After exploring the Hastings area and walking over to Fairlight Glen along the cliffs he felt inspired to take up a passion of his that he had started at school and continued at college: the idea of television. Baird worked tirelessly throughout 1923 developing his work. The editor of *Broadcasting* magazine and the chief research engineer of the BBC visited Baird in Hastings. He was also contacted by Will Day, the owner of a London cinema with whom he entered a partnership to work on transmitting images. By the end of 1923 Baird has successfully done this. The month of January in 1924 saw Baird appear with his creation

There are secrets to be discovered in Queens Arcade and in the architecture.

Ornate plasterwork in Queens Arcade.

in the *Hastings Observer* newspaper and the national *Daily News*. It was in this year that news of his experiments reached far and wide, and many invitations flooded in for Baird to give talks about his work.

However, in the summer of 1924 Baird suffered an accident as a result of an electrical fault with part of his work; a shock sent him across the length of his workshop and he was found lying on the floor with burns and damaged equipment. This incident resulted in his landlord asking him to leave his workshop and so Baird returned to London to continue his work. He still made frequent visits back to Hastings and gave lectures at the White Rock Theatre, saying he 'always had pleasant memories of Hastings. I owe a lot to your air and sunshine'.

It was in Hastings in 1929 that the town became the first to honour Baird for his achievements. A plaque was placed in Queen's Avenue during a ceremony, which Baird himself attended. This plaque can be viewed today for anyone passing along this part of the town. Let us hope that the scientific advancements of this incredible man are never forgotten.

The Jerwood Gallery, The Stade

Any exploration of the old town and The Stade will bring you to an unusual and striking building located on Rock-a-Nore Road. This is the award-winning Jerwood Gallery, which opened in March 2012 and sits next to the fishing beach in Hastings' historic old town. The gallery became a charity in 2017 and is home to the Jerwood Collection of Modern and Contemporary British Art and a varied temporary exhibition programme championing the best of British painting.

It was designed by Hana Loftus and Tom Grieve. Interestingly, the building is covered in over 8,000 black tiles – known as mathematical tiles – that were glazed in Kent and are similar to those used in the construction of many of the houses in the old quarter. The gallery has founds its home among the local fishing industry and works with the local community on projects.

As well as paid staff, the gallery also has a team of over sixty volunteers who assist visitors to the gallery and help them to make the most of their experience.

The incredible work on display at Jerwood Gallery.

The view from one of the many picture windows at Jerwood Gallery.

The gallery café, Webbe's, overlooks the fishing beach and has an outside sun terrace offering panoramic views of the coastline. It's a fantastic location for a coffee, lunch or afternoon tea. The café has a few secrets of its own too: tables are made from wood from the original Hastings Pier and ceiling lamps are made from lobster pots. There are several large windows placed around the building that provide remarkable views over the old town, encapsulating the unique heritage of the fishing heritage of Hastings.

The design has a strong emphasis on sustainability, with the building creating 60 per cent less CO_2 per square metre than an average museum of comparable size. The gallery is almost all naturally ventilated. Eleven 120-metre-deep ground source probes provide all the cooling and 60 per cent of the heating for the building. Solar thermal panels heat most of the building's water and rainwater is collected and recycled for use in the toilets – a remarkable construction.

Sir Quentin Blake had the following to say about Jerwood Gallery in 2017: 'What I could never have imagined is that someone would build an art gallery at the end of my road which is within walking distance, that's wonderful, and it's such a nice art gallery as well. It's absolutely what one could wish.'

The view from the Jerwood, showing the houses of the area close by.

The unique mathematical tiles used in the construction of Jerwood Gallery.

Hidden Gardens

You will find parks and gardens all over the borough of Hastings and St Leonards. One of these gardens is in a secret place: Linton Gardens. Located in a residential area just a stone's throw away from the centre of Hastings, it offers a delightful open space and sanctuary for locals and visitors alike. During the 1940s an open-air theatre was created here, which provided a much-loved and popular venue in the centre of beautiful gardens.

DID YOU KNOW?
In the central part of Alexandra Park you will find the trunk of an old oak. This was taken from the submerged forest at the end of the pier in 1871.

Alexandra Park is the main park in the borough, and runs alongside an ancient stream that flows from old Roar Ghyll to the sea at Harold Place. One of the first garden areas to be set out was Shirley's Pond, which was created by a local man named Mr Shirley in the 1830s. This area can be found at the main entrance to Alexandra Park, by the railway bridge and the boating lake in St Helens Road. In 1972, plans were drawn up to enlarge the park and include local woods and a reservoir. Part of the woods date back to smuggling times and, walking through them today, it is not difficult to imagine smugglers lurking among the trees in days gone by.

Alexandra Park, the largest park in the borough, has many lakes in its design as well as flower beds and tree-lined areas – a much-loved green space..

The park was redesigned in 1878 by Robert Marnock, a well-known landscape gardener who had worked on projects such as Regent's Park Gardens. The Prince and Princess of Wales formally opened Alexandra Park on 29 June 1882 and two trees – an oak and a beech – were planted near the bandstand to mark the occasion. Since then the park has been extended; it now runs for 2.5 miles and covers 110 acres. It offers beautifully laid out rose and flower gardens, wooded walks, leisure and sporting activities, and peaceful lakes and streams. Magnificent plants and trees have been planted throughout the park, offering great beauty to the area.

The parks today are greatly enjoyed by residents and visitors alike, and host many events throughout the year.

White Rock Gardens is one of many open spaces in the borough.

Cinema, Queens Road

Today you will find the town's cinema located on the corner of Albert Road and Queens Road, in the heart of the commercial district. The building was known previously as the Odeon cinema and the Gaiety Theatre, and was originally built as a private venue in 1882. It was closed in 1932 and converted into the cinema that we see today. Little has changed to the exterior of the building and if you glance up you will see the impressive ornate decoration it has to offer.

The grand regal exterior to the modern cinema in Queens Road.

Cinema De Luxe

Another magnificent building is what is known today as the Deluxe, which offers amusements and bingo to its customers – how many of these have ever wondered about the origins of the building they are in? The best way to appreciate this venue is by crossing over the road and looking at it from this perspective. You will be met with ornate windows, a balcony overlooking the road below, and domed roofs.

In the past this building has been known as the Empire Theatre and the Royal Marine Palace of Varieties. Decorated heavily with ornate baroque-style plasterwork, this building was constructed to be noticed and stand out.

It is easy to imagine how this magnificent building was once the heart of local society. People came from all around to watch and listen to the varieties performed here including short plays, recitals and singing.

The Stables Theatre, High Street

From the outside this theatre looks like a relatively modern building, which is a correct assumption as it was built in 1956. However, what you will not be immediately aware of is its hidden history, for what you see is actually a combination of the more recent construction and old stables used by troops during the Napoleonic Wars. The Old Town Preservation Society helped to save the ancient stable block and preserved it as part of today's Stables Art Gallery and Theatre. Many of the original parts of the building were able to be saved – including many of the original beams – and used in the new construction, when extensive work was carried out. The theatre was opened in 1959 by Sir Ralph Richardson and since that time the venue has become second to none, putting on many professional performances and shows over the years.

Fairies

Do you believe in fairies? Many people from Victorian times felt that they shared their world with these mysterious creatures. Many fairies are said to dwell at a place very close to Hastings known as Fairlight. This area of the town has been known by various other names over the years including Pharos Lit, meaning 'lighthouse'. The name Fairlight may also be a corruption of words meaning 'bracken clearing'.

The country park at Fairlight covers 5 miles of wonderful rural splendour with glens and fantastic bays and is an ideal place to walk. This area is also known as the Firehills, possibly because of the bracken fires in the summer months or because of the huge fires that were kept alight here to guide ships safely ashore.

Over the years there have been many reported sighting of tiny people, standing no more than 8–12 inches tall with small wings on their backs. They have appeared to many, often watching people working or picnicking with their families, and are said to approach the humans with little or no fear whatsoever. Many tales of these fairies were told by shepherds, and farmers were often said to have been helped by the fairies. Fairies rewarded people who worked hard on the land and were kind to nature by leaving silver coins in their boots during the night. Fairies are said to like spending their time in peaceful places surrounded by beautiful natural surroundings; perhaps that is why they are so frequently seen at Fairlight.

9. Education and Religion

By the end of the eighteenth century Sunday schools in Hastings had become very popular and were effective in teaching reading and the principles of religion. They were cheap and did not interfere with the weekdays. The first Sunday school in Hastings was held at the chapel in the Croft from 1805 onwards. Records state that by 1831 over 11,000 children had attended the school. On 18 November 1835 a national school was opened on the East Hill, which offered schooling at the cost of 1d a week to the children's parents. Further schools also opened up, including the British School for Girls in 1835, located in Waterloo Passage, and the Boys' British School in Wellington Square.

DID YOU KNOW?
The vicar of All Saints' Church was hanged in 1586 for forging an order of preservation to the living.

There seems to have been a large number of private schools throughout the town from the early nineteenth century, despite the state education on offer. There was one in particular that, despite its small size, helped to shape some of the most notable men in the town in the nineteenth century. This school, located at No. 117 High Street, was managed by Miss Lydia Barrow from 1837 and she remained there until her death in 1874 at the age of eighty-four. The house itself was built around 1770 and owned by the surgeon Samuel Satterly who rented it to Miss Barrow.

Often, some of the most beautiful places are those you least expect. Forgotten, hidden churches that are walked past each and every day often blend into the busy times of modern life. However, open a door of one of these churches and you are often greeted with the past and awe-inspiring architecture and design.

One of the place names in the town named after significant events.

Church in the Wood, St Leonards

The Church in the Wood in Hollington, St Leonards, has long been a popular place for worship and celebrations. Hidden away on the outskirts of the town, it is among many of the secret and forgotten churches that many locals are not even aware exist. There are a number of accounts that the church has existed as far back as 1080, with the original structure being located a few hundred feet away from its current site today.

There is a local story about the building of the church. It tells of a young priest who chose the location for the original church, but for three consecutive nights all the building work that had been done during the day was pulled down and the priest was back to where he had started. He was mystified by this action and was told by locals that this was the work of the Devil. The priest was told to build the church in the wood instead, so he began building again in an ideal spot located among the trees. Each morning he returned expecting his work to have been undone, but this was not the case and the church continued to be built. The church was called the Church in the Wood as it was situated among the trees, far away from the gaze of the Devil.

The church has attracted visitors since the mid-eighteenth century and was lit by candles right up until 1977 when electricity was installed. It has what is known as a Devil's doorway, which was the northern entrance to the church. This would have been opened during confirmation and communion services so that the Devil could be let out. One of the oldest bells in the town is housed in the bell tower of this church and is said to date from around 1371. The oldest tombstone in the graveyard dates back to 1678, but no one knows who is buried here.

DID YOU KNOW?
At a church in the nearby village of Crowhurst you will find an ancient yew tree said to be over 3,000 years old.

Iden Church, near Rye

Venture towards the medieval town of Rye, some 9 miles to the east of Hastings, and you will find the village of Iden. You will come across a wonderful church in this village, which has gargoyles that look down from their tower on the marshes where the sea used to proudly roll. The little church has stood for over five centuries. Fragments of the angels who once looked down from the doorway are fading away, but two ancient king posts still stand holding up the roof. A brass can still be found that is dedicated to William Seller, who looks out across the nave where his flock gathered to hear him preach 500 years ago.

Old St Helen's Church, The Ridge

Today, Ore is very much part of Hastings but once upon a time it was very much its own village. You can find an ancient and ruined church if you look carefully, lost among trees down a grove of pines. The ruin is now roofless with little left, but offers a sanctuary for the explorer slightly off the beaten track along the area of Hastings known as the Ridge. Old tombs are encased with ivy and moss and stone faces are worn out. However one thing does remain which has been preserved in the new church close by. Is it the oldest but one of all civilian brasses in Sussex, being the portraits of an unknown couple who died here in the closing years of the fourteenth century. Preserved here also are the old church's registers dating from 1558.

Old St Helen's Church, The Ridge.

Bohemia House School

Bohemia House in Summerfields was a magnificent farmhouse dating from 1818. It was built in a wonderful manor house style with an imperial-style staircase constructed from pine and wood. It has vast amounts of elaborate detailing throughout the large and impressive building. The estate included a coach house, which would have housed two coaches and up to six horses with ample sleeping accommodation for the coachmen. There were also mock Roman baths built to make the most of the natural springs in the area; these still exist in the woods today, along with an icehouse. In the days before refrigerators, icehouses were packed with ice from local ponds to keep food fresh. They were constructed as a deep brick-lined well with a domed roof; sometimes they were built into banks of earth to give added insulation. Also on the estate were vast gardens, which included a private walled garden, vegetable gardens and beautiful ornamental gardens. The house was reached from the main road, where two lodges were built: North Lodge and South Lodge. South Lodge survived until 1999.

In 1903 Bohemia House became Summerfields Preparatory School for boys aged between eight and thirteen. It was a school for sixty years and many famous people were educated and prepared for life here, including the Marquess of Blandford and the King of Jordan. This house was described by many who attended the school as an ideal location and environment to learn in. During the Second World War the school was used as the Town Hall of Hastings, reverting to a school at the end of the war. It was a great loss to many people when in 1972 this historic house was pulled down, as it was a well-loved landmark in the town.

The Old School House, All Saints' Street. One of many historic schoolhouses in the old town.

The Old Ragged School, No. 39 Tackleway

Ragged schools were set up in nineteenth-century Britain and offered free education to children from poor families to teach them skills in trades to get started in life. Schools in London helped over 300,000 children between 1844 and 1881. Children were provided with meals and taught the skills of trades such as shoemaking and printing. They were also taught reading and writing skills. These schools were initially started for boys, with girls' schools opening later. Many of them were run by volunteers in buildings such as churches and other public places.

Charles Dickens supported these schools and campaigned to change the appalling conditions of some of them. It was Dickens' own experiences of the ragged schools that led him to write *A Christmas Carol* and *Oliver Twist*. You will find one of these schools at No. 39 Tackleway, which was opened in 1863 to provide free schooling for the poor of the area.

Just along from the ragged school you will find All Saints' Church, standing majestically at the top of All Saints' Street. This originally dated from the 1400s, but it was rebuilt later due to war and the elements. It is one of the oldest churches in the area and has a wonderful churchyard to explore.

Pett Church

Located 4 miles outside of Hastings you will find the village of Pett. Today Pett consists of residential properties and at Pett Level there is a wonderful haven for many types of birds and other wildlife. Pett Level is a great place to explore and when the tide is out you can see parts of an ancient forest that once stood here.

The Church of St Mary and St Peter was built in the 1860s and is well known for its large gargoyles that stare down at visitors. It is said that the gargoyles come alive after dark and follow people home and if the victims realise they are being followed, the gargoyle turns into the Devil himself. This sight is said to be so evil that the victims are severely shocked and drop down dead on the spot.

All Saints' Church, All Saints' Street.

George MacDonald

George MacDonald was born in 1924 in Aberdeenshire. His working life started out as a lecturer in the church and then he turned to the writing of hymns, novels, poetry and fairy tales. He moved to Hastings in 1857 for health reasons (as so many people did) and it was here that he set up home at No. 27 Tackleway in the old town. During his time in Hastings he wrote a book called *Phantastes*, which was to later inspire C. S. Lewis and J. R. R. Tolkein with their work.

In 1858 he left Hastings for London; however, he returned some ten years later with a somewhat larger family than he left with: some eleven children! They all lived at Hollaway House, which was located off Old London Road. It was from here that he wrote *At the Back of the North Wind*.

He was well known for his keen interest and involvement with local activities and was the founder of the Hastings and St Leonards Philosophical Society in 1858. He also gave lectures throughout the town.

George passed away in 1905 at Ashted in Surrey; however, he achieved a lot in his writing career, publishing over sixty books, many of which are still in print today.

Christchurch, St Leonards

In the centre of modern St Leonards you will find Christchurch standing proudly. What you see today replaced the smaller original building of 1860, which became part of the parish rooms to the south of the church. It was designed by Sir Arthur Blomfield and was consecrated in 1875. It was designed as a statement of the Oxford Movement, which began in the 1830s and influenced many famous priests. In this church there were no rents payable for the pews as it was wished that the church be as inclusive as possible.

Christchurch, St Leonards.

St Mary Star of the Sea Church, High Street, where Catherine Cookson was married.

Holy Trinity Church is very much at the heart of the town community, located in the Trinity Triangle or America Ground area.

10. Food and Drink

If you think of a day trip to Hastings you cannot imagine it without fish and chips served up in paper and eaten strolling along the promenade or in one of the many fish and chip restaurants in the town. But how many think about the beginnings of this dish, now considered one of the nation's favourites? So, how did it all begin? By the late 1850s the potato was the 'in' food and being served up baked whole in its skin, in slices or even stuffed, and a few years later they appeared in tins and were used in soups. Mrs Beeton recognised these new ideas and spoke of the French trend of frying raw potato strips, which in the 1870s became known as chips. With ships returning from the seas with vast quantities of fish, the humble dish of fish and chips was born and soon became very popular among the working class as it was sold for a penny. Its popularity has continued up and down the country to this day, Hastings being no exception.

As well as ties with seafood, Hastings also has a rich heritage of breweries and public houses. At one time there were forty-seven inns and pubs in the old town area alone (some 1 square mile). Sadly, there are less than half of these today as many were turned into residential houses and apartments. However, you do not have to venture too far around the area to unearth some secrets.

Ye Olde Pump House, George Street

Despite its name and appearance, Ye Olde Pump House opened as a pub as late as 1956. The building's footprint dates back earlier than 1890, however, when the Barnes family were documented to have lived here until 1943. The structure of the building is mostly original, including the pebble decoration to the front. Local historians have been very interested in some of the windows, which show great age and originality. The timbers that make up the frontage were brought from bombed sites in the High Street and from a local shipwreck.

The building was originally three separate dwellings: a cobbler's shop at the front, a private residence called Cliffside House to the top half, and Norton House was the back dwelling immediately under the rock face. This backed onto the famous caves of the West Hill where there is evidence of an arched entrance to a cave – now blocked up. It is suggested that this is where the original pump was sited that drew water from a natural spring and was well known locally for its clarity and purity. This pump was preserved and can now be seen affixed to the front of the pub as an ornament.

The cobbler's shop – named it Stoakes and Carey – was owned by brothers Sidney and William Carey. In 1953, however, a fire destroyed the whole building. In 1956 it was completely rebuilt and the frontage redesigned by a Canadian called Anthony Newman.

Ye Olde Pump
House, George
Street.

The cobbler's and Cliffside House lay derelict from 1943, with casual occupation from
the war by a carpenter/builder. Sidney Carey then sold up to the Goodhew family (well
known for their hotels and catering) and in 1982 it was acquired by a large brewery.

Anchor Inn, George Street

This old pub today is as popular as it has ever been. Up until the seventeenth century, the
area all along this part of the old town used to come up to the bottom of the cliffs. This pub
was therefore originally built on stilts, allowing small boats to anchor themselves to the

The Anchor Inn, George Street. This pub was built on stilts so that boats could anchor themselves easily.

structure. George Street suffered from flooding right up until the 1920s when the Bourne clearances began and the sea defences were constructed. (The Bourne clearances were instigated by the local council to improve the town by removing the ancient medieval properties, making way for progress and development.)

Another secret not many know is that before there was a courthouse in Court House Street the back bar of the Anchor Inn was used as a courtroom, and many local criminals were sentenced here for crimes such as theft and unruly behaviour. This may explain why the figure of a tall man wearing a dark suit and top hat is often seen in the back bar; there used to be a portrait of an old judge hanging in the Anchor Inn and the figure looks very much like him. Some say that the judge's spirit returns to make sure that the locals are behaving themselves.

The Stag Inn, All Saints' Street

This inn in All Saints' Street dates back to the sixteenth century and is a history lover's delight. Just walking past you would not know the secrets that this pub contains. It is home to a collection of mummified cats and rats that were found in a fireplace when some work was being carried out. The animals were said to have been put there in the 1500s by the black witches of Hastings to ward off evil spirits.

Secrets also lie in the back bar area in the shape of two mysterious black marks that have appeared on the wooden floor. No one knows how they got there and they are known locally as the witches' footsteps. Over the years attempts have been made to get rid of them by sanding the floor and even replacing the wooden floorboards, but the marks always reappear as if by magic.

Cinque Ports Inn

The Cinque Ports Arms in All Saints' Street is one of around a dozen historic inns in the old town, all of which have fascinating stories surrounding them. At one time there were around forty or fifty inns in the old quarter, but many of these disappeared in the Bourne clearances. Some pubs of yesteryear are now private houses or shops; for example, the Roebuck Inn in the High Street is now the Roebuck House doctors' surgery and the Kicking Donkey in Hill Street is a private house.

The inns in the old town have served many purposes. A lot of the old town pubs were used as hiding places for smugglers and their goods. Their deep dark cellars made them ideal places, with and entrances to tunnels connecting properties and churches all over the area. The Dolphin Inn on Rock-a-Nore was very busy during the smuggling era, especially on a Sunday morning after the large boats had come ashore with all their goodies. The Dolphin was the smugglers' first port of call and became one of the most notorious pubs in the old town, with many reports of riotous behaviour from the drinkers and sometimes even the landlord.

Inns have long been used as meeting places. The Swan Inn at the southern end of the High Street, on the corner of Croft Road, was a very grand coaching inn and once the centre of the community, holding many social events over the years. Sadly, the Swan took a direct hit during the Second World War and sixteen people were killed; the little garden on the site was created in memory of the victims.

There is one fascinating old inn that is known as the Ole in the Wall, although no one can be sure why it was given such a name as its location is nowhere near the area known as Hastings Wall. Today the former inn can be found in Hill Street as a private house. During its life it was run as a greengrocer's shop and had a licence for the sale of beer.

Right: Ole in the Wall – one of the many old pubs that once existed in the old town.

Below: The Kicking Donkey in Hill Street was once a pub.

Left: The Cinque Ports Inn, All Saints' Street. This was once the site of the ancient Wealden Hall House, which was destroyed by fire.

Below: The Fisherman's Institute was originally set up to try and offer an alternative to the many inns and alehouses for local people.

11. The Arts and the Artists

Literature, like art, is timeless. The streets of Hastings are ever present with the spirits of writers who walked, talked and wrote here. Here and there visitors will see a little blue plaque on the outside of houses, which state who once resided within the walls.

For centuries Hastings has attracted writers and artists of all sorts. Many wonder what drew them to this town and what they hoped to find. Were they inspired by the history and heritage the town offers? Many stay for a short while, while others make it their home.

Three hundred years ago John Taylor – 'the Water Poet' – spent three days in Hastings and wrote the following of the town:

> Much to that town my thankfulness is bound
> Such undeserved kindness there I found
> Three nights we lay there and three days we spent
> Most freely welcomed with much merriment

Sinnock Square can be found by following a twitten from the High Street or from Croft Road. Narrow passageways lead you into a small courtyard edged by picturesque cottages from all ages. This square has been the inspiration for many artists who have made Hastings their home or have featured the area in their work. Many have described it as one of the old quarter's secrets that few visitors or even locals are aware of.

DID YOU KNOW?
Of the many passageways around the old town, Sinnock Square was once known as Tripe Alley owing to the number of meat sellers once found here.

LEWIS CARROLL
(1832 - 1898)
Writer and Scholar
was a frequent visitor
to this house,
the home of his aunts
the Misses Lutwidge
O. H. P. S.

Plaque showing Lewis Carroll's connection with the town.

East Cliff House

Many of the houses around Hastings have associations with unusual people. East Cliff House can be found at the bottom of All Saints' Street. It was designed and built by Edward Capel in around 1761 at the cost of £5,000. He held the office of Censor of Plays and it is said that he copied out the whole of Shakespeare's works ten times. Garrick also visited Capel here and brought with him a cutting from the poet's mulberry tree at Stratford-upon-Avon.

DID YOU KNOW?
Notable residents have included: the poets George Macdonald who lived at Halloway House, Old London Road; the painter T. S. Cooper; actors Edmund Kean and Elliston, who performed at the first Hastings theatre in Ore; and the novelist Mark Rutherford, who lived at No. 9 High Wickham.

Dickens Cottage can be found in the High Street. While it is not believed that Charles Dickens lived here, it is said that he visited his mother at this house on numerous occasions.

12. In Times of War and Conflict

From early medieval times the town of Hastings has been protected from attack from the sea by the sea wall, which was built along the front of the old town, originally across the Bourne Valley between the two hills. Sadly little remains of it today and those who do cast their eyes on it would not pay it any respect for its provenance. Part of the wall can be found along the edge of the beer garden of the Royal Standard public house. There is also a small fragment where High Street and George Street meet, and another part runs alongside where the modern flats were built – named Hastings Wall.

The town was badly in need of defences, and in 1339 and 1377 the French made their mark on Hastings. It was during one of the French or Dutch invasions that St Clements Church in Croft Road took a direct hit. If you look up at the front belfry window you will see two round objects set up high in the stone walls. The round stone object on the right-hand side is a cannonball that was fired by an invader, and the one on the opposite side was put there by locals to even out the effect and make it look more appealing.

Whenever you mention Hastings to someone from outside of the town, they instantly say, 'Oh the place where the battle took place in 1066'. This is a common misconception as the battle did not actually take place in the town of Hastings, but rather some 5 miles to the north at a place that owes its name to the event that shaped history: the market town of Battle.

DID YOU KNOW?
During the Second World War, St Clements Caves were used as air-raid shelters for people of the town.

St Clements Church, Croft Road. Look up and see if you can spot the cannonballs set up high in the belfry.

Battle

A visit to the site of the Battle of Hastings is not one many can do without being moved. You can walk through the noble gateway and across the grounds and find yourself at the place where Saxon England died. It is said to be the place where King Harold fell. The battle between Harold and William changed the shape of British history, but there is so much more about this area and town to be discovered.

One monumental piece of architecture is the church, the foundation stone of which William the Conqueror raised in honour of his victory over Harold. While surrounded by the frantic modern world outside, it is possible to sit in the grounds of the abbey and imagine what it must have been like when the men who remembered this famed king sat and talked and ate there. A fountain garden was laid out here over 300 years ago by Sir Anthony Browne and a glorious Cedar of Lebanon rises where it is said William the Conqueror slept after the battle ended.

It is often easy to forget that following the most famous battle in British history the town of Battle grew and flourished into the market town you see today. It is also easy to forget that monks made this place their home and had richly productive gardens in the abbey grounds. Little sadly remains of the Norman church of Battle, namely just the round arch in the chancel and the columns on which the thirteenth-century arches rest. The church, standing among fine trees a short distance from the abbey, is an impressive place yet seldom thought about. Its chief possession is the monument near the altar of Sir Anthony Browne, who is depicted lying in armour with the Order of the Garter and his wife beside him wearing a necklace. The tomb is a massive monument and richly sculptured on almost every inch, with winged angels and little animals decorating each side. Henry VIII gave the abbey to Sir Anthony in its glory days, who turned it into a house.

DID YOU KNOW?
The Battle of Hastings, 14 October 1066, was not fought in Hastings but at a town some 5 miles inland, which now bears the name Battle.

It is said that the work of the building is that of a great master who fled to England from Italy after breaking Michelangelo's nose. He was known as Torrigiano and he also made the tomb for Henry VII at Westminster Abbey.

In the graveyard of Battle's church there is a stone on the grave of a man who held a very honourable record for service. He attended the abbey as a boy and was a faithful servant there for over ninety years.

If you venture up the High Street in Battle you will come across Battle Museum, which is full of interesting artefacts and information. One secret that has been kept there for thousands of years is an axe head that is thought to have survived from the Battle of Hastings – the only artefact of the battle ever found. The lack of finds is due to a combination of acidic soil and scavengers picking up all usable weapons after the battle, but it is a bit of a mystery all the same. In 1951 Battle and Hastings celebrated the Festival of Britain. The local history society thought of asking people to contribute anything old they had found and an exhibition was put on. This axe head was among over 1,000 items contributed. Battle Museum was set up to care for the objects after the festival was over. So, the museum have kept this a secret for over sixty years.

The axe head was found just off Marley Lane in Battle (on the way to Hastings) while it was being widened. It is thought that this area was very likely the Saxon front line when they met the Normans coming up from Hastings at 9 a.m. on Saturday 14 October 1066. The axe head has been assessed by experts at the Wallace Collection in London, who confirmed it is of the ninth to twelfth century. The V-shaped fitting for the long handle is also typical of Saxon weapons of the time – it's not an ordinary woodman's axe. The Saxons fought without horses so would have been able to wield a weapon like this; it was less easy for the Normans, who were usually on horseback. We had a replica made in 2016 by Hands on History and they concluded the same as the Wallace Collection, adding that it has softer metal inside designed to be a shock absorber. At the end of a 4-foot ash handle this would have been a deadly weapon, designed to be swung heavily to chop off heads and the legs of Norman horses, a reminder of the brutality of that conflict.

Battle is also known in history for its connections with the production of gunpowder in the area. Many believe that it was gunpowder from here that was used in the famous 5 November 1605 plot. Each year Battle hosts a huge event around 5 November to mark its special place in history.

An ancient axe. (Kindly provided by Battle Museum)

Guy Fawkes history surrounds the town of Battle.

The Cinque Ports

It is often forgotten that Hastings is one of the five towns that make up the Cinque Ports (the others being Hythe, Romney, Dover and Sandwich). It is thought that these five towns originate from the fact that fishing boats from them made their way to Great Yarmouth every herring season, becoming known as the Five Ports – this was a long time ago, many believe before the Battle of 1066. From then their association grew and, as there was no Royal Navy, these boats and ships were the only available source of vessels when they were required. Edward the Confessor is said to have offered these five towns certain privileges in return for the use of their ships, but whether this is true or not in unclear as there are no sources to back this up. The ports are first mentioned in a charter of Henry II in around 1155.

In return for certain privileges the ports had to provide fifty-seven ships, each with a crew of twenty-one men and one boy for fourteen days per year when required by the king. Should they be required to provide further service, then this would be paid for.

By supplying these vessels the towns could command potential power and influence and were able to negotiate with the Crown and were rewarded significantly. One of the privileges awarded was that all freemen of the ports were named barons. As well as holding this title they were also exempt from certain taxes, and were able to organise the great Herring Fair at Yarmouth and control the foreshore. There was also one final gift that still remains today: the 'honours at court'. At the king's coronation the towns provided barons to carry and hold the canopies during the processions, and were seated at the banquet afterwards. This privilege has changed somewhat over the years but does still exist – to a lesser extent – and is certainly worthy of being included in these secrets about the town.

Hastings' coats of arms has its own story to tell. It is different due to the lion in the middle, but there is no evidence to confirm the date this was created. The common seal of the town is that of a Cinque Ports ship running down another vessel and dates from around 1300, so it is thought the coat of arms design would have been done date after this.

Battle of Sidley Green, Bexhill

A visit to Sidley will greet you with a small high street in a suburb of Bexhill. However, if you have an eye for history you will no doubt spot the New Inn set upon Sidley Green. The old inn is quite a stark contrast against the rest of the more modern surrounding architecture. The New Inn dates back to the 1700s and was a favourite haunt of the smugglers. In the 1700s it was known as the Eight Bells. Sidley was the site of the Battle of Sidley Green in 1828, when a gang of local smugglers came up against the coastal blockade guards.

Battle Abbey

Close to the Royal Victoria Hotel in St Leonards you will find a large flat stone. Many believe that this is the exact spot where William, Duke of Normandy, landed in 1066 before the famous battle took place; it is said that he used the large stone as a table for his pre-battle meal. Others say that there are connections with King Harold here and that he is buried beneath where the stones lies today. When Harold's body was found on the battlefield, William ordered it to be interred on the foreshore at Hastings in the belief that as he had guarded and protected these shores during his life, he could continue in death. He then ordered that Harold's body be buried under the stone. The stone later became a marker used by the Hastings smugglers; many cargoes have landed within its vicinity without bothering the customs guards.

Buildings of Battle
Abbey are now
a school.

Look closely at who is peering down at you from the abbey's windows.

The Duke of Wellington

Major General Sir Arthur Wellesley was born on 1 May 1769 and died 14 September 1852. He would later become known as the Duke of Wellington and was knighted for serving a very successful term in India from 1796 to 1805. He is one of our most well-known historical figures, famous for his leading military and political roles and he also served as prime minister twice. However, his connections with Hastings are less well known.

He was posted to Hastings in 1806 to take command of the infantry. His troops were based locally while he stayed at No. 54 High Street, which was used as his headquarters. Today this building is home to a popular antique centre, yet to look at the building and architectural style of the property it is easy to imagine the Duke of Wellington surveying the High Street and looking down from the large windows onto life in the street below.

The Duke married in April 1806 in his home town of Dublin and brought his new bride to Old Hastings House in Hastings. Sadly this no longer exists, but it would have been situated where Old Humphrey Avenue is. Old Hastings House was described as being a Palladian mansion and stood high on Tackleway with extensive gardens. Across the road from No. 54 High Street there once stood a grand coaching inn called The Swan Inn. It was here that a large public dinner was held in 1806 for the Duke. In 1829, the Duke was given the title of the Lord Warden of the Cinque Ports.

Around the town today there are many areas commemorating the Duke of Wellington; for example, Wellington Square in the town centre, Wellington Mews and even a public house in the High Street bears his name. There is a second public house too that was named after him, which can be found in a suburb of the town known as Silverhill. The pub – The Duke – was built in 1868 (despite the date of 1895 being etched on the windows) and architecturally is very little altered from those days – it is one of the few pubs in Hastings to still retain a separate public and saloon bars. The pub was originally named the Duke of Wellington, but was shortened to The Duke to avoid any confusion between the pub in the High Street. The pub's sign at The Duke still depicts Arthur Wellesley, Duke of Wellington.

No. 54 High Street was once the residence of the Duke of Wellington.

Hastings War Memorial, Alexandra Park.

A plaque telling of the Duke of Wellington's connections with the town.

Bibliography and Acknowledgements

Brown, *Haunted Hastings* (Stroud: Tempus Publishing, 2006).

Colquhoun, *Taste the Story of Britain through Its Cooking* (London: Bloomsbury, 2007).

Dyer, *Hastings and St Leonards – A Brief Story* (Hastings: 1958).

Dickson Wright, *A History of English Food* (London: Random House, 2011).

Langlands, Goodmand and Ginn, *Edwardian Farm* (London: Pavillion Books, 2010).

Manwaring Baines, *Historic Hastings* (London: Parsons Limited, 1955).

The author would like to thank the following people/organisations for permission to use copyright material in this book: Alastair Hendy, Adrian Hall (Battle Museum), Margaret and Robert Emeleus, Jason Neale (Photostrada), Peggy Hensher (Pegasus Photos), Jacqui Baughurst, Ion Castro and Kevin Boorman.

About the Author

Tina Brown was born and brought up in Hastings, East Sussex, and since 1992 has researched, designed and guided tours around Hastings' old town, Rye and other areas in the UK and also Bulgaria. Tina has always had a passion for history and for bringing the past to life in an interesting and memorable way. Tina has long believed that if you visit a historic house, castle or ancient town then you should come away asking questions and wanting to know more about the place, the people and the events that have shaped its life.

As well as an interest in history, archaeology and historic gardens Tina also has a keen interest for tattoo history which she is currently researching for a book and has recently completed *The History of Gin,* which is due out later this year.

The author, Tina, leading a history tour in Hastings.